The Life Intense

LETTING BE VOLUME I

The Life Intense

A Modern Obsession

Tristan Garcia

Translated by Abigail RayAlexander,
Christopher RayAlexander and
Jon Cogburn

EDINBURGH
University Press

Edinburgh University Press is one of the leading university presses in the UK. We publish academic books and journals in our selected subject areas across the humanities and social sciences, combining cutting-edge scholarship with high editorial and production values to produce academic works of lasting importance. For more information visit our website: edinburghuniversitypress.com

La Vie Intense: Une obsession modern by Tristan Garcia © Autrement, Paris, 2016
English translation © Abigail RayAlexander, Christopher RayAlexander, Jon Cogburn, 2018

Edinburgh University Press Ltd
The Tun – Holyrood Road,
12(2f) Jackson's Entry,
Edinburgh EH8 8PJ

Typeset in 11/13 Bembo by
IDSUK (DataConnection) Ltd, and
printed and bound in Great Britain.

A CIP record for this book is available from the British Library

ISBN 978 1 4744 3711 0 (hardback)
ISBN 978 1 4744 3713 4 (webready PDF)
ISBN 978 1 4744 3712 7 (paperback)
ISBN 978 1 4744 3714 1 (epub)

Contents

Series Editor's Preface

This English translation of *The Life Intense*, the opening third of a nearly completed trilogy entitled *Letting Be*, is the second book by Tristan Garcia to appear in the Edinburgh University Press Speculative Realism series. Garcia (b. 1981), a native of Toulouse now employed at the University of Lyon, is already among the best-known philosophers of his generation. His lengthy work *Form and Object: A Treatise on Things*, which appeared in this series in 2014, captured the public imagination with its rare blend of systematic rigour and sensitive insight into the intimate features of contemporary human life. *Form and Object* also inspired one of the most important commentaries on any continental philosopher in recent decades: Jon Cogburn's *Garcian Meditations*, which appeared in this series in 2017. In that masterfully argued book, Cogburn makes a strong case for Garcia having already secured his place in the history of philosophy, while also linking his work with that of the daringly offbeat analytic philosopher Graham Priest (b. 1948). Cogburn has not yet had his fill of Garcia, and returns as his co-translator once more, this time in the company of Abigail and Christopher RayAlexander.

As we are reminded in the Translators' Introduction below, the notion of intensity has had an important place in Garcia's thinking from the outset. *Form and Object* was famously split into two parts, the first dealing with anything *n'importe quoi*, or 'no-matter-what' (a technical term in his system). In this connection Garcia gave us the flattest of flat ontologies, compared with which even the claim of Object-Oriented Ontology (OOO) that all real and fictional things are objects was made to look too conservative: for Garcia, after all, even parts and portions of objects count as 'no-matter-what' to no less an extent than mid-sized everyday objects. The rigorous auster-ity of the analyses early in *Form and Object* have reminded both me and others of Hegel's *Science of Logic*. By contrast, the second part of *Form and Object* turns from the ascetic poverty of things to the colourful determinacy of what Garcia calls 'objects'; here we find a sequence of cultural analyses more reminiscent of Hegel's *Phenom-enology of Spirit*. In *Garcian Meditations*, Cogburn clarifies why this twofold description of entities as both things and objects is a thrill-ing high-wire act that enriches Western philosophy. Although I will not attempt to gloss Cogburn's argument here, there is no question that *intensity* is the key new ingredient in the second part of *Form and Object*, the one that allows Garcia to shift from flat austerity to a lush forest of concrete insights. Nonetheless, Garcia would be the first to admit that intensity receives insufficient treatment in that book. *The Life Intense* is, in no small part, an attempt to make good on his obligation to the reader to say more about this pivotal con-cept, which he treats in a way rather different from that of Gilles Deleuze and his followers.

The Life Intense is so compellingly written that I need not bela-bour its argument here. Garcia gives us a highly original definition of modernity in terms of the prominence it grants to *electricity*, viewed originally as a means of escaping the cold objectivity of modern science: recall the crucial role of this phenomenon in the philosophy of nature of F. W. J. Schelling (1775–1854), who was certainly no mechanist. The theme of electricity animates Garcia's fascinating discussion of the history of ethical intensity running from the libertine, through the romantic, on up to the adolescent: a newly prominent historical character who already played the star-ring role in *Form and Object*. In this connection, *The Life Intense* offers what is surely the most profound meditation ever attempted on the philosophical significance of the electric guitar: these few pages alone are worth the price of the book! Garcia also draws a useful distinction between the electric and its de-intensified version, the *electronic*, the latter being our apparent destiny as the modern age of intensity runs up against its limits. Another memorable moment of the book comes in Chapter 5, with its discussion of the three 'ruses' we employ in an attempt to maintain intensity: variation, acceleration, and what Garcia terms *primaverism*, meaning especial devotion to our first experience of anything.

As always when reading Garcia, the reader has the sense of an author who sees everything at first-hand, effortlessly melting down any clichés that obstruct his path, usually before we even realise that they are clichés. He is erudite in the classical sense, referring whenever needed to ancient or medieval currents of thought, but is also a peerless observer of the most recent cultural trends, whether in music, sexuality, or sport. As a rule, I find myself happier – more optimistic and energised – after having read even ten or so pages of his work. But unlike the fearsome first half of *Form and Object*, the pages of *The Life Intense* fly by so quickly that one or two sittings may be enough to absorb this book for the first time.

In closing, I would like to thank the translators for their consistent enthusiasm for this project, and for their success in leading it to a wonderfully readable result. I look forward to their work on the next two volumes of Garcia's trilogy.

Graham Harman
Ankara
January 2018

Translators' Introduction

One could argue that this book does not need a Translators' Introduction. Tristan Garcia's paramount virtue as a literary stylist is
his ability to manifest accessibility without sliding into breeziness.
And, unlike his systematic *Forme et objet: Un traité des choses*, *La Vie
Intense* neither relies on technical vocabulary nor contains densely
imbricated metaphysical argumentation. But readers beware! The
text that are you about to read is Janus-faced, exoterically a work
of what some English-speaking philosophers call 'critical theory'
and esoterically something much deeper.

Critical Theory versus Speculative Metaphysics

All great philosophers more or less unconsciously react against
the model of humanity presupposed by their fellow creatures. For
some, such as Nietzsche, this reaction is very close to the surface of
every book. For Marx and Marxists it *is* the surface. But less mon-
omaniacal philosophers also pen individual books explaining what
is distinctive, and distinctively awful, about the historical moment
in which they find themselves. Prior to Garcia's *La Vie Intense*,
our most recent paradigm examples are Søren Kierkegaard's *The
Present Age*, Miguel de Unamuno's *Tragic Sense of Life*, C. S. Lewis's
The Abolition of Man, and Herbert Marcuse's *One Dimensional Man*,
all four of which we continue to read to understand the authors'
cultural milieus as well as our own. And from this perspective,

La Vie Intense is a familiar sort of book of a type produced inter-
mittently in the Western philosophical tradition, an analysis and
evisceration of the ethical norms enforced by the society in which
the philosopher finds him or herself.

When read as an instance of this genre, the first three chapters
of *La Vie Intense* should be viewed as presenting the ideological
prehistory of what is distinctive about present humanity. According to Garcia, the contemporary philosophical cult of intensity can
only be understood as a reaction against the most important early
modern philosophers taking the universe to be a giant machine
devoid of intrinsic purpose. And it is no accident that such theoretical views were ascendant just as the human being was being
reduced to a cog in the mechanical human hybrid known as the
factory. The person tasked with repetitively turning a lathe for
over half of his or her waking hours has as little connection to the
factory's purpose as does the mechanical universe to the hopes and
dreams of an increasingly distant God.

As Garcia presents our prehistory, electricity was experienced
as the great exception to mechanism. It flowed wild, romantic,
and unbound, the life force underlying and animating what would
otherwise be dead matter. It moved our muscles and ignited the
storms in the sky, a concrete image elevated in the fight against
the mechanical.

La Vie Intense's first three chapters are the story of electricity's
breakthrough and then ultimate domestication. In science proper,
raw forces such as the electromechanical are no longer exceptional.
Once we discover their fundamental laws, we manipulate them just
as the early moderns manipulated timepieces and factory workers. And the metaphysical systems of intensity developed by process
philosophers such as Nietzsche, Bergson, Simondon, and Deleuze
follow suit, only succeeding by failing. For intensity is metaphysical electricity, and as such shares the same fate. What was supposed
to be an exception to the rational schemes of the mechanists and
substance metaphysicians became, in the work of the process philosophers, the norm. Our greatest metaphysicians thus devoted their
lives to developing rational accounts of what was supposed to be
an exception to rational accounts. And, as Garcia argues, a universe
where everything is intense is a universe where nothing is intense.

Garcia's prehistory of electric humanity is not mere stage setting, as one of his central conceits is that the fate of our theory of intensity is mirrored at the practical level. Just as our attempt to think intensity ends up having us think of intensity as non-intense, our attempt to live intensity ends up gutting our lives of intensity. And these reflected movements happen according to the same logic. The constitutively exceptional cannot become the norm. Yet the ethics of consumer capitalism dictates that we attempt to make it so.

When reading *La Vie Intense* as a work of philosophical social criticism, Chapters 4 to 6 form its heart. Chapter 4 traces the evolution of the archetypes of those who seek novelty and excitement above all else, initially the aristocratic libertine and the bourgeois romantic, and now the adolescent rocker whose ethos has in various ways colonised all of contemporary culture. Chapter 5 describes the ruses of which we avail ourselves in increasingly futile attempts to maintain intensity: variation, acceleration, and primaverism ('springism', or the worship of first times). But all such ruses follow the logic of addiction, leading to collapse and burnout. Chapter 6 describes and analyses this burnout. For Garcia, it is an inevitable result of the way that thought and life (which includes both action and affective experience) interact. Thought involves identifying disparate things as being of the same kind. But, in a brilliant discussion of improvised music, Garcia describes the manner in which novel experiences must become re-identifiable in thought. And as such, they are then experienced as no longer really novel.

No denizen of the contemporary West will make it through Chapter 6 without looking deeply at her or himself and the cultural milieu in which she or he wallows. And, if Garcia were the kind of grifter that populates our milieu, he would conclude with a set of easy instructions to liberate us from our pathology. Surely we need only take a radical leap of faith, or perhaps reject faith and embrace our role as legislators of morality, or perhaps commit ourselves more fully to the revolution. Or retreat into yoga and meditation. Plant medicine. Alternatively, let us imagine Sisyphus happy, happy with his new tattoo and Apple products, ironic affectation the flower on the chains of his boring job, pictures of yet another mountain ascent posted to social media, etc., etc., etc. Feh.

No! Garcia is not a philosopher of easy answers. In Chapter 6, he reinterprets ancient spiritual traditions in terms of their relation to the ethics of intensity. Contemplative wisdom traditions, associated with the East, are understood as attempts to reduce intensity to zero. Traditions promising salvation, canonically marketplace versions of Christianity and Islam, are understood to promise maximum intensity. But, according to Garcia, both of these prove illusory. Here Garcia perhaps unknowingly recycles the Buddhist critique of the Hindu wisdom realisation that Atman is Brahman, that the self is totality. But if the self is totality, that is, everything, then there is no self. Likewise for salvation, any successor being of myself capable of being cradled by God for eternity would not be me, since I am a creature finitely bounded by time, space, and mental capacity. But then both the ethics of intensity and the revival of pre-intensive ethics end up undermining life. And since the ethical for Garcia centrally concerns how to live, both the ethics of intensity and its rejection are self-undermining. Aporia.

In his concluding chapter, Garcia returns to the antagonism between thought and life, and argues that the task of ethics is to fight the reduction of thought to life as well as the reduction of life to thought. But if this is the task, then a work of philosophy, a work of thought, which of necessity reduces everything to thought, cannot complete the task. Garcia's critique of contemporary humanity does not come with a set of instructions for how to save oneself, not even the paradoxical meta-instruction to come up with a set of instructions yourself, as Sartre essentially mandates in *Existentialism is a Humanism*. This too is self-defeating for Garcia. No, much like the ending of Alejandro Jodorowsky's *The Holy Mountain*, Garcia releases his readers into the world with no answers and the promise of neither wisdom nor salvation. But, with Jodorowsky, if we have not obtained immortality, at least we have obtained reality.

Thus, we have *La Vie Intense*'s exoteric Janus-face, an examination of the human condition at this point in history. And fair-minded readers will conclude that Garcia has our measure. Our civilisation enforces a way of life that renders us all addicts in varying stages of 'recovery'. Even those of us who think we are revolting against it, from existentialists to religious fundamentalists to video game players to born-again hippies to members of twelve-step programs to vegetarians to all of the lost, wandering souls gazing down into their cell phones ... all of us are operating in the space made possible by the ethics of intensity. Garcia definitely has our measure.

And if this were the entire book, there would be no special difficulty in translating it! Again, there is no especially forbidding technical vocabulary, the French is accessible without being breezy, and the argumentative structure is not especially circumabulatory. The only minor problems here arise from genre conventions that result from the high level of literacy among beneficiaries of the French educational system and broader literary culture. *La Vie Intense* contains many references likely to be lost on readers who reside in countries with education systems that do not particularly value the humanities and populations who do not as a whole read literature and non-fiction on public transport. Thus, at the risk both of pedantry and of spoiling some of the fun of reading the book, we have added citations and notes explaining many of Garcia's allusions.

But, and here is the much bigger issue, the allusions are not just to historical tropes such as the delicacies of Capua or literary classics such as Rimbaud's poetry or *Les Liaisons dangereuses*. The entire text is simultaneously an esoteric allusion to Garcia's encyclopaedic work of metaphysics, *Forme et objet: Un traité des choses*, also available in Edinburgh University Press's Speculative Realism series as *Form and Object: A Treatise on Things*. And the allusions are always just allusions. Nowhere in *La Vie Intense* does Garcia explicitly mention or cite *Forme et objet*. But the allusions are overwhelming, so much so that we confidently state that, in spite of the accessibility of its exoteric reading, *La Vie Intense* would be untranslatable to someone not deeply steeped in *Forme et objet*.

Note that this does not mean that the reader who has not read *Forme et objet* faces an insurmountable hermeneutic circle. Part of *La Vie Intense*'s brilliance is that it scans beautifully and rewardingly to a reader who has no inkling of its other face. But this other face, the sense in which it is a continuation of and commentary on *Forme et objet*, is just as important. And it is in the service of helping the reader and future scholars make out the outline of this hidden face that we include many of our notes as well as this Introduction.

Intensity in *Form and Object*

Form and Object consists of two books, the first of which presents a pure ontology, that is, an account of the formal properties of all entities, every kind of thing from bodies of water to tables, to trees, to dreams, to geometrical figures, to square circles, to bacteria and the creatures they inhabit, everything, every thing. Book II, on the other hand, consists in twenty-six regional ontologies, accounts of what is distinctive to specific types of entities such as time, humanity, and value. While Book I is presented as a set of numbered propositions and commentary, Book II is divided into twenty-six chapters, each of which provides a history of our thinking about the kind of entity in question. As Graham Harman has quipped,[1] it is as if Garcia reversed Hegel's original order, starting with the *Logic* and then appending to that the *Phenomenology of Spirit*. But unlike at least most readings of Hegel's *Phenomenology*, Garcia's genealogies do not end in reconciliation, but in some combination of aporia, contradiction, and tragic choice.[2] For example, Garcia argues that death places irreconcilable normative demands on us. When confronting one's own death, one should manifest stoicism. But realising this undermines our ability to respond appropriately to others' deaths. We should not be stoic about others' deaths, but should grieve. Nor should we limit our comforting of the afflicted to the counselling of stoicism. What is appropriate for oneself is inconsistent with what is appropriate for others.

It is as if Garcia has strengthened the traditional saying, 'Woe unto those who seek justice upon others and mercy for themselves.' From a Garcian perspective, we have an obligation to inconsistently seek justice upon ourselves and mercy for others. And this is not a clever formulation to be denuded of its power by some ultimate reconciliation either in history or the minds of philosophers; rather, as is so often the case with Garcia, it is reflective of a constitutive contradiction in reality.

---

[1] Harman, 'Object–Oriented France'.
[2] For an account of how this works in Book II, recapitulating Book I's basic model of being, see Cogburn's *Garcian Meditations: The Dialectics of Persistence*.

Book I of *Form and Object* describes a world that permits such contradictions and aporia. In common with other object-oriented ontologists such as Harman, Garcia is motivated by the paradoxical impetus to describe what reality must be like such that it constitutively eludes our ability to describe it.[3] Philosophers such as Harman can be seen as responding to this paradox by characterising metaphysical description as of a different kind than empirical description. In fact, for Harman, metaphysics has more in common with art than science.[4] Philosophers such as Garcia, on the other hand, take the paradox to reflect the inconsistent nature of reality.[5]

Irrespective of their distinct meta-philosophies, for both Harman and Garcia the manner in which reality resists our attempts to characterise it actually ends up giving us insight into what reality is like apart from our characterisations of it. For we ourselves are part of reality, and thus to the extent that we have any special insight into ourselves, the experience of entities resisting us is the experience of entities resisting one another. Harman is thus able to wage a guerrilla metaphysical struggle using the resources of Heidegger's and Husserl's phenomenologies, but now in the service of metaphysics.[6] The Heideggerian manner in which objects withdraw from our epistemic and practical grasp is a model for the (non)interaction of all objects with one another.

---

[3] Chapter 1 of Cogburn's *Garcian Meditations* describes in detail this anti-reductionism, and Chapter 3 presents a formal derivation of the paradox that results from it. Interestingly, wide swaths of continental philosophy can be differentiated in terms of how the philosophers in question can be interpreted as responding to this paradox.

[4] See Cogburn's 'Aesthetics as First Philosophy: Sense Making after Speculative Realism' for a discussion of how the paradox mentioned in the previous note sets in bold relief Graham Harman's novel meta-philosophy, which in important respects should be seen as the culmination of what A. W. Moore calls the 'creative tradition' in metaphysics, spanning from Nietzsche through Bergson, Carnap, and Deleuze.

[5] For other canonical sources of this tendency in contemporary thought, see Graham Priest's *Beyond the Limits of Thought* and Paul Livingston's *The Politics of Logic: Badiou, Wittgenstein, and the Consequences of Formalism*. One of the major conceits of Cogburn's *Garcian Meditations* is the construction of this tradition, with Garcia its most recent avatar.

[6] For Harman's externalisation of Heidegger, see *Tool Being: Heidegger and the Metaphysics of Objects*. For the analogous treatment of some of Husserl's key insights, see *Guerrilla Metaphysics*. And for an accessible introduction to the metaphysics produced by combining the two interventions, see *The Quadruple Object*.

For Garcia, on the other hand, the manner in which entities elude our comprehension gets externalised in a radically different way. While Harman's model of being is in essence withdrawal, for Garcia, entities are differentiators between that which they comprehend and that which comprehends them. While comprehension can be epistemic for creatures like us, for Garcia comprehension includes a variety of relations, including spatial containment, mereological constitution, and being an instance of. Understood this way, the idea that every object or thing comprehends some other entities and is comprehended by other entities should be commonplace. What is distinctive about Garcia's view is that an object or thing just *is* that which differentiates between the entities it comprehends and those which comprehend it.

The first major consequence of Garcia's differential model of being is the manner in which it fits into object-oriented ontology's anti-reductionism. If Garcia's model is correct, then all successful reductions are eliminative. For example, if it really were the case that all of the truths about a desk were really truths about the physical parts that constitute the desk (which the desk comprehends, in Garcia's terminology), then there is a sense in which there is no desk, just the desk's parts. For Garcia, on the other hand, what makes the desk an entity in its own right is that it is the bearer of what analytical philosophers refer to as 'emergent properties', properties of the desk (and for Garcia properties comprehend their bearers) that are in some strong metaphysical sense not properties of the desk's parts.[7] So for Garcia to say that the desk is a differentiator between those entities which it comprehends and those entities which comprehend it is to say that the desk is the locus of genuinely emergent properties.

The second major consequence of this differential account, one that sets the stage for much of *Form and Object*'s Book II, is the

---

[7] A version of object-oriented ontology which directly privileges emergent properties is presented in Levi Bryant's *The Democracy of Objects*. For Bryant, the virtual proper being of an object is its novel capacity to exhibit properties when interacting with other objects. This is anti-reductionist to the extent that such properties are genuinely emergent. Of course this only makes sense if there is a good account of what genuine metaphysical emergence amounts to. In this context, see especially Jon Cogburn and Mark Silcox's 'The Emergence of Emergence: Computability and Ontology'.

inevitability of ubiquitous aporia. This is because our explanations
of an entity typically proceed by either explaining the behaviour of
the entity's parts or by explaining the entity's relationships to other
things. Harman calls these two kinds of explanations, respectively,
undermining and overmining.[8] If Garcia is right that entities are differentiators in the sense that a successful reduction would be a demonstration of non-being, then it follows that our best undermining
explanations will be frustrated by our best overmining explanations,
and vice versa. And, indeed, this kind of aporia is nearly universal in
Book II of *Form and Object*, most of the chapters of which consist
in parallel stories: an undermining, naturalistic one of the history
of our best accounts of the behaviour of the physical parts of the
manifestation of the kind of entity in question, and an overmining,
sociological one concerning how that kind of entity affects and is
affected in turn by the kinds of objects to which it is related.

To return to our example of death, Garcia describes the grim
history of how our physical definitions of death have changed
along with our changing abilities to keep otherwise incapacitated
people alive and to revive people we would have previously taken
to be dead. But if death were merely a matter of non-beating hearts
and electrical activity, there would be no death. For death is the
death of an organism, which as an entity differentiates between the
(here physical) entities that compose it and the entities (here sociological, political, and spiritual) which it helps to compose. And as
we understand better and better the processes that compose death,
we must now face the question of the status of a person (as of this
writing, fictitious) with a destroyed body but whose memories and
personality have survived after uploading into a digital computer.
For Garcia there is no answer to this. Not because we haven't carefully defined our terms, but because the nature of reality makes it
impossible for the definition of terms to solve such problems. Like
all entities, death itself is a site of antagonistic struggle between that
which it comprehends and that which comprehends it.

Book I of *Form and Object* contains much more of fundamental
philosophical import. For example, Garcia understands each entity

---

[8] The canonical discussion is in Harman's *The Quadruple Object*. For a discussion of Garcia
in this context, see Chapter 1 of Cogburn's *Garcian Meditations*.

as bifurcating into two modes, objects and things, and uses this bifurcation to attempt to avoid the Scylla and Charybdis of metaphysical atomism and holism, and the related opposition between substance and process ontology. He puts forward novel treatments of numerosity, matter, world, and the dispute between nominalism and Platonism. Garcia's ontology is wildly promiscuous in the 'flat' sense that to be is to be determined, a premise that entails that even contradictory entities such as square circles have being. While these themes are treated explicitly in Book I, they are all instantiated over and over again in various ways in Book II.

In Garcia's order of explanation, Book II's regional ontologies all presuppose in various ways the major insights and metaphysical categories from the pure ontology of Book I. Strangely, though, the most ubiquitous metaphysical category in Book II is intensity, which is not treated at all in Book I. For example, Garcia's chapters on time, life, beauty, truth, and goodness all constitutively involve intensity. For Garcia, an event is a present fact, and the presence of a fact is something which is more or less intense, with the relative intensity of a fact's presence determining its place in the time sequence, present facts being the most intensely present.

Intensity then crops up again in Garcia's chapter on life, with the difference between non-living and living entities being a function of the intensity of the difference between that which the entity comprehends and that which comprehends the entity. While all entities are manifestations of this difference,

> the emergence of living things is the *intensification* of this irreducibility. The property of irreducibility of a thing to what is in this thing, is this thing, and composes this thing accounts for the stratification of the entire material universe into levels. The emergence of living things can be thought from the fact that this irreducibility has a particular *intensity*.[9]

Thus, as with intensity's role in determining the relative pastness of events, for Garcia entities are more or less alive depending on the intensity of their irreducibility.

---

[9] Garcia, *Form and Object*, p. 192.

Intensity is also a key factor in Garcia's chapters on each of the Thomistic God's perfections: beauty, truth, and goodness. For Garcia, beauty is the intensification of an object itself. If life is the intensity of the difference between that which comprehends an object and that which an object comprehends, beauty is the intensity of the entity itself, which is the differentiator. When we judge an object as less beautiful than it should be, we are comparing it with another version of itself which is in fact more itself than it actually is. And truth is the intensity of the relation of comprehension between an entity and that which comprehends it. Finally, goodness is determined by a definition of an entity being good for something, where something is good for something else to the extent that it renders that second thing more intensely itself. Thus, for Garcia, goodness is in the end parasitic upon beauty. That which renders the world more beautiful is good.

It is impossible to convey in a short introduction exactly what Garcia means by these invocations of intensity.[10] In each of the cases, he provides a more or less exhaustive reconstruction of the history of our concept of the kind of entity in question, drawing in the end on contemporary, cutting-edge empirical and conceptual work. For example, the characterisation of life as intensifying irreducibility is solidly built on a discussion of our most recent understanding of the role that homeostasis plays in organisms. In this manner, we get an implicit understanding of intensity in Book II of *Form and Object*. Garcia's encyclopaedic discussions add meat and friction to the philosophical claims. By witnessing what intensity is doing, we get some sense of what it must be.

Nonetheless, nowhere in *Form and Object* does Garcia ever tell us what exactly intensity is. It is merely what you add to the objects from Book I to get the world we live in. But what is it itself? The ubiquity of intensity in Book II strongly suggests that it should have been handled in Book I, which serves as a transcendental explanation of the main theoretical concepts used in Book II's genealogies. For example, comprehension is similarly

---

[10] The reader could do worse than avail her or himself of Chapters 8 and 9 of Cogburn's *Garcian Meditations*, albeit those chapters fail to do justice to the richness of Garcia's genealogies.

ubiquitous in Book II, and Book I does provide an account of it. Why not intensity?[11]

When being charitable, we suspect that this is the genesis of the sniffling gripe we have personally heard from many Deleuzians to the effect that the problem with *Form and Object* is that it does not contain an account of intensity. When being uncharitable to our Deleuzian friends, we sometimes suspect that the complaint is really that Garcia does not adopt Deleuze's account of intensity. In either case, one cannot begin to struggle with the esoteric reading of *La Vie Intense* unless one reads it as answering both the charitable and uncharitable reading of the Deleuzian grouse.

La Vie Intense's Aporia

According to Garcia, the manner in which intensity constitutively plays a role as an exception to thought renders the project of providing a metaphysics of intensity oxymoronic. This is one of the main reasons he does not adopt something like a Schopenhauerian or Nietzschean or Bergsonian or Simondonian or Deleuzian process philosophy of intensity.[12] That is, in Chapter III of *La Vie Intense*,

---

[11] A longer discussion would connect Garcia's placement of an account of intensity both within and beyond *Form and Object* with similar tropes in continental and analytic philosophy. American continental philosophers tend to associate poststructuralism generally, and Derrida's deconstructionism in particular, with the idea that any system contains an element that is also of necessity excluded from that system. Intensity is surely this element with respect to *Form and Object*'s system. But the idea predates poststructuralism, as the exact same conceit was presented by Deleuze in 'How Do We Recognize Structuralism?' as one of the key planks of structuralism itself. Deleuze traces it back to Claude Lévi-Strauss. In *The Politics of Logic*, Paul Livingston is able to formally articulate the point with respect to Deleuze and Derrida by using Gödel's incompleteness theorems. In *Garcian Meditations*, following Priest and Livingston, Cogburn shows that Russell's Paradox provides a universal form for many such arguments involving inconsistent inclusion and exclusion.

[12] Though it is not the only one. See especially the discussion of Garcia's critique of both substance and process philosophy (especially with reference to the Putnam–Parmenides argument) in Chapter 5 of Cogburn's *Garcian Meditations*. The problem is that the tradition of process philosophy that culminates in Deleuze (to be differentiated from that of Whitehead and Latour) either begs the question by invoking individuated beings in the account of individuation, and hence not really treating relational processes as fundamental, or (here, arguably, with Whitehead and Latour) entails a British Hegelian monistic night where all cows are black. The Putnam–Parmenides argument is one route to this conclusion.

Garcia argues that to treat intensity as metaphysically basic is to no longer treat it as intense. With respect to Deleuze, the supposedly non-individuated processes underlying the realm of individuated objects end up being question-beggingly infected by individuation.[13] And Garcia argues that such would be the fate of all attempts to think intensity. Since thinking for Garcia constitutively involves the twin acts of 1) re-identifying entities as being the same over time and 2) differentiating entities in terms of whether they are instances of the entities which comprehend them, it follows that thinking necessarily presupposes the kind of flat ontology treated in Book I of *Form and Object*.

La Vie Intense's contribution to meta-metaphysics would not be aporetic if it were merely an argument that metaphysical accounts of intensity are always doomed to a kind of failure. In fact, Garcia already suggests in *Form and Object* that all metaphysical accounts are doomed to failure because metaphysics constitutively, and inconsistently, treats the world as an entity in the world. Yet for Garcia metaphysics is still necessary because of the failure of Kantian and post-Kantian anti-metaphysical attempts to fence in the epistemically safe. For Garcia, and Graham Priest and Hegel for that matter, limits only make sense relative to what is beyond them. But then the very notion of an absolute limit, here fencing off a realm supposedly free of metaphysics, is intrinsically contradictory. The upshot of all of this is that we cannot really do metaphysics, yet we must!

La Vie Intense presents an aporia because Garcia attacks both the attempt to think intensity, which he takes as a paradigmatic attempt to theoretically reduce life to thought, as well as attempts to reduce thought to life. That is, the injunction of our age, to unthinkingly value intensity above all things, is just as self-defeating as the attempted metaphysics of intensity, and for parallel reasons.

---

[13] This is perhaps clearest with Deleuze's progenitor Gilbert Simondon, who takes the process of the formation of crystals out of fluids as his paradigm metaphor for individuation out of processes. Simondon explicitly notes that crystal formation requires a seed, which is already a non-fluid object! If we are to follow the metaphor, as we are supposed to, we conclude that individuation requires individuated objects. But such a philosophy cannot be one where what is really real is intensive processes, as basic individuated objects are being directly appealed to. See Cogburn's review of *Gilbert Simondon: Being and Technology*.

Garcia's analysis of the ethics of our age, beginning in Chapter IV, is an analysis of the manner in which life cannot, in Garcia's sense, eliminatively reduce thought. For as thinking beings (and Garcia includes animal cognition in his definition of thinking) our experiences cannot but be cognisable.[14] I experience a work of free jazz as a work of free jazz. But Garcia meticulously argues that this basic fact damns all intensity to become less intense. An ethics devoted to intensity, the reduction of thought to life, is ultimately just as self-defeating as a metaphysics grounded in it.

As a work of meta-metaphysics, *La Vie Intense* consists in three chapters concerning the reduction of life to thought, three chapters concerning the reduction of thought to life, a chapter showing how traditional ethical approaches (wisdom and salvation) have been changed by humanity's detour through intensity in ways that render them unable to cope with the failure of the ethics of intensity, and a concluding chapter stating our aporetic condition with respect to thought and life.

Our task is not to elucidate and evaluate the arguments in Garcia's texts, but rather to render visible both of their faces. In the service of this, we merely have one more point. It should be noted that Garcia's aporia actually has a fourfold structure, one that is slightly obscured by the text's layout. When the reader gets to the final chapter, she or he sees that Garcia is critiquing both the reduction of thought to life and the reduction of life to thought. But because of the manner in which Garcia's esoteric focus on *Form and Object* informs his presentation, the reader might not be aware that each reduction has both a theoretical and practical aspect (see Table 1). For example, the practical reduction of life

---

[14] Here is another place where Garcia's book connects with important strains in contemporary analytic philosophy. John McDowell's *Mind and World* is an extended meditation on what to make of the Kantian claim that there are no unconceptualised experiences. According to McDowell, both the Kripke–Wittgenstein paradox and Wilfred Sellars's 'Myth of the Given' problematic arise from problems with the Kantian claim (which McDowell does not reject). If our experiences are always already conceptualised, how do experiences possibly exert normative force with respect to our conceptual schemes? But isn't it possible for a conceptual scheme to be bad? What could this possibly be if there are no non-conceptual experiences by which to assess our concepts? As briefly explicated below, there are deep connections between Garcia's aporia concerning thought (which is the conceptual for Garcia) and life (which encompasses experience) and McDowell's problematic.

Table 1

	Thought reduced to life	**Life reduced to thought**
Theoretical	Relativism about truth and knowledge, e.g. Nietzsche's perspectivalism[1]	Process philosophy, e.g. Nietzsche's will to power[2] [critiqued in Chapters 1–3]
Practical	Ethics of intensity, e.g. marketplace existentialism[3] [critiqued in Chapters 4–6]	Wisdom and salvation, e.g. Stoicism and various spiritual traditions [critiqued in Chapter 7]

[1] Cf. Nietzsche, 'On Truth and Lies in an Extra-Moral Sense'.
[2] Cf. Nietzsche, *The Will to Power*. Lee Braver's *A Thing of This World* contains an excellent discussion of the various approaches in the literature to the tension in Nietzsche's perspectivalist relativism about truth and knowledge and later metaphysical pronouncements which themselves seem to presuppose a kind of realism inconsistent with relativism. Braver shows that the incoherence runs throughout Nietzsche's work. For example, the view that morality involves useful falsehoods presupposes a fact of the matter about truth and falsity. This, of course, flatly contradicts the equally Nietzschean view that truth is nothing more than a form of usefulness.
[3] We are somewhat wary of stating it thus, as Garcia never cites Sartreanism, though from our notes the allusions will be clear.

to thought consists in attempting to live a life devoid of intensity while the theoretical reduction is the attempt to incorporate intensity into one's metaphysics. The fact that an overwhelming proportion of Garcia's discussion concerns the theoretical privileging of thought and the practical privileging of life, combined with the fact that he does not discuss the theoretical privileging of life, somewhat obscures the true structure of the aporia. But Garcia's final chapter, where our predicament is presented as the struggle against both reductions, needs to be understood as defending the claim that this is a theoretical and practical struggle, and both *Form and Object* and *La Vie Intense* need to be read as part of this struggle.

Likewise, one might respond to Garcia's aporia by simply counselling that we not reduce either term to the other. But if we realise that these are theoretical and practical tendencies, we will better understand Garcia's claim that these reductions are in some sense *necessary* impossibilities. As thinking and living creatures, the precipices he describes cannot be filled in. Perhaps we can balance ourselves along their shared spine, but they are not going to disappear.

Concluding unsemantic postscript

In closing, we would like to return to Graham Harman's insight that *Form and Object*'s structure is the reverse of that followed by Hegel, with Garcia's Book I corresponding to Hegel's *Logic* and Garcia's Book II corresponding to *The Phenomenology of Spirit*. If we examine why Hegel wrote the *Phenomenology* first we will actually gain insight into why *La Vie Intense* begins a new trilogy, followed by the just-published *Nous*, and to be finished by a projected work of ontology.

According to standard accounts such as Frederick Beiser's *Hegel*, the conclusion of Hegel's *Phenomenology of Spirit* is what makes it possible for him to write the *Science of Logic*. The latter book is an unabashed exercise in metaphysics of the sort thought to have been prohibited by Kant. Kantians were not supposed to be able to claim knowledge about reality as it is in itself. Philosophy could not be dogmatic metaphysics, but must stay on this side of the phenomenal/noumenal distinction, theorising about the structure of appearances and criticising those who transcend appearances. However, if the *Phenomenology of Spirit* is successful, then Hegel's conclusion that thinking equals being ensures that being itself is knowable. For the knowledge prohibited by Kantians is actually, after the *Phenomenology*, a form of self-knowledge after all.

In a certain way, Book I of *Form and Object* is far more Kantian than one might otherwise think, as long as we replace the subject with world. If Kant's task in the *Critique of Pure Reason* was to understand the way the mind must be structured so that we can have the experience that we do, Garcia's task is to understand the way the world must be structured so that we can live the way that we do (remember that for Garcia, experience falls on the 'life' side of the thought/life divide).

But notice that Garcia's transcendental order faces a problem in common with Kant, a problem that Hegel, if successful, would not face. The task of Hegel's *Phenomenology* is to explode Kantianism from the inside. Thinking of limitations as limitations forces us to inconsistently claim knowledge of what lies beyond those limitations.[15] This is of no special philosophical import when the limitation is that imposed by the wooden fence ringing your garden. But with respect to absolute limitations, such as what can be known, conceived, or described, paradox ensues, as knowing, conceiving, or stating the limitation forces us to know, conceive, or state what is supposed to be beyond the limits of knowledge, conception, or statement. Hegel, on standard interpretations, responds to the paradox by undermining the appearance/reality distinction in favour of appearance. The unknowable is after all knowable, if only to itself, a universal process which we find ourselves participating in as little specks of God-mind, matter becoming spirit, and never so paradigmatically as when we do the kind of speculative metaphysics undertaken in Hegel's *Logic*. Metaphysics is the material universe becoming conscious of itself.

While Garcia clearly shares Hegel's view of limits,[16] he does not use the paradox to motivate the Hegelian voiding of the reality side of the appearance/reality distinction. Instead of justifying the practice of metaphysics with absolute idealism, in Book I of *Form and Object* Garcia presents his pure ontology in transcendental terms. In order for the things we experience and think about to be experienceable and thinkable, they must be as described in Book I. As noted, this methodology is a speculative extension of Kant's own procedure of attempting to characterise how the mind must operate so that we can have the kind of experiences and thoughts we do.

The Garcia of *Form and Object*'s Book I is a speculative thinker. He is describing the formal properties of the world, not our

---

[15]This is also the structure of the first half of Quentin Meillassoux's *After Finitude*, according to Graham Harman's reading in *Quentin Meillassoux: Philosophy in the Making*. Joshua Heller and Jon Cogburn use modal logic to formalise Harman's interpretation in 'Meillassoux's Dilemma'. For this kind of move as a running theme in German Idealism, see Frederick Beiser's *The Fate of Reason: German Philosophy from Kant to Fichte* and *German Idealism: The Struggle against Subjectivism, 1781–1801*. In the Hegel chapter of *Beyond the Limits of Thought*, Graham Priest was the first to explicate it in terms of a Russellian inclosure paradox, though his focus is on the treatment of infinity in Hegel's *Logic*. The inclosure nature of Cogburn's object-oriented ontology paradox in *Garcian Meditations* makes even more pronounced the connections between German Idealism, Speculative Realism, and Object-Oriented Philosophy.

[16] See the section titled 'Limit' (pp. 138–41) in *Form and Object*.

experience of the world. Nonetheless, and notwithstanding his commonalities with Hegel on limit paradoxes, the transcendental status of his thoughts about the world forces him to confront a distinct problem facing Kant, that of the *quid facti*. One of the earliest essays on Kant's *Critique of Pure Reason*, Salomon Maimon's *Essay on Transcendental Philosophy*, contains a brief but devastating criticism of Kant's transcendental methodology. Basically, even if we grant that Kant has correctly described how we must (*quid juris*) presuppose the mind to be in order for us to have experience, this only has philosophical relevance if experience does indeed exist (*quid facti*). And Maimon's second main argument, involving problems with Kant's intuition/concept distinction, leads us to doubt that experience, at least of the sort Kant alleges, does exist.[17]

The analogous *quid facti* problem for Garcia is clear. Even if we grant that Garcia has correctly described how we must (*quid juris*) presuppose the world to be in order for us to have thoughts about the world, this only has philosophical relevance if thought does indeed exist (*quid facti*). One might thus take Book II of *Form and Object* to be, among other things, an existence proof for the thought elucidated in Book I. But a sceptical reader might view Garcia's thought as a Procrustean bed, with the genealogies in Book II cut and stretched to fit.

Note that the amount of insight in each chapter of Book II amply demonstrates the obnoxiousness of the sceptical reader. But to appeal to the insightfulness of Book II is in effect to say that the reader should compare her or his own life with Book II's discussion. We thus are invited to evaluate Garcia's thoughts about life and the presupposed thoughts about thought in terms of whether our own lives confirm or disconfirm these thoughts.

---

[17] Maimon's arguments here make him the dialectical progenitor to the issues raised in note 14 above. See Meir Buzaglo's *Solomon Maimon: Monism, Skepticism, and Mathematics*. Note that, for Maimon, an infinite intellect such as God would not have experience, but would operate purely at the level of the conceptual. Empirical experience is just an aspect of our finitude, and the distinction between empirical intuition and conceptual concept is one of degree for Maimon. Buzaglo shows that Maimon's view about this actually stems from a brilliant insight into the manner in which analytic geometry was allowing geometric proofs without the use of spatial figures. Harman's speculative Heidegger can actually profitably be interpreted as an externalised Maimonism here, with the distinction between scheme and content depending upon which sensual qualities are manifested when an object interacts with another.

But is this even possible? A running theme of *La Vie Intense* is the sense in which our experiences are always already conceptualised (cf. the analytic philosophers discussed in note 14). This is why we cannot reduce thought to life. But, in addition, if there is no unconceptualisable experience, it is entirely unclear how we evaluate a conceptual scheme in terms of experience. So *Form and Object's quid facti* problem remains unsolved, and if this were all there were to say on the matter, unsolvable.

Fortunately, with respect to the *quid facti*, we are surely saved here by the fact that life is not reducible to thought. For Garcia, life is not merely concept-laden experience, and thus there is more to assessing a conceptual scheme than measuring it in terms of the experience informed by that scheme.[18] We must attend to the vague dissatisfaction that leads to rebellious ways of life such as libertine, romantic, and rocker. We cannot help but think this dissatisfaction, giving rise to the ultimately self-defeating theoretical cult of intensity. But life is the activity too, and activity that can be seen to be rational in retrospect is often initially a correct, if not therefore rational, response to something inchoate. And it will ever be, because thought is not reducible to life. As we write this, the inchoate is birthing new archetypes in reaction to our electronic reality. If literate humanity survives the transition, our best philosophers will think these changes too.

So *La Vie Intense* does do something similar to Hegel's *Phenomenology* with respect to the possibility of metaphysics, albeit in a much less triumphal manner. By presenting aporetic genealogies of our theoretical attempt to reduce life to thought and our practical attempt to reduce thought to life, Garcia is able to paint both as inevitable failures, not merely inevitable in the sense that they are doomed, but inevitable in the sense that we cannot do otherwise. Whereas for Hegel, metaphysical thinking is saved by the affirmation that reality is radically thinkable (since it is all appearance), for Garcia, metaphysical thinking is saved by life's resistance to being fully

---

[18] Harman has a distinct way out of this, since for him aesthetic experience forms a non-discursive non-conceptual basis for normative assessment. With respect to metametaphysics, Harman's view ultimately involves assimilating metaphysical explanation to norms appropriate for aesthetic evaluation. See Cogburn's 'Aesthetics as First Philosophy: Sense Making after Speculative Realism' for an account of how this works with respect to inclosure paradoxes, though the same aspects of Harman's system also produce a solution to the issues noted in note 14 above.

captured by thought. This resistance is not a generic failure resulting in scepticism, but rather consists of specific failures that inchoately prompt new ways of living, which thinking then catches up with, albeit denuding them of their force upon completion of the seizure.

Interestingly, Hegel's late *Encyclopedia of the Philosophical Sciences* reverses the order of his earlier works, now beginning with a *Science of Logic* as Book I. So, in this respect, the early Garcia's ordering in *Form and Object* is akin to Hegel's later ordering. And, even more interestingly, Garcia's *La Vie Intense* is the first work of a new trilogy, whose name we have translated as *Letting Be*. Garcia's trilogy reverts to Hegel's earlier ordering, as it will conclude in a treatment of ontology. This, of course, makes perfect sense if we are correct that *La Vie Intense* plays a meta-metaphysical role analogous to Hegel's *Phenomenology*. And we also have a good sense of the excitement of Hegel's contemporaries as we ourselves witness the flight of Garcia's thought through *Nous* and beyond.

We would like to thank Emily Beck Cogburn, Philip (Andy) McLean, Charles Pence, François Raffoul, and Eamon Roach for their friendship, solidarity, and philosophical insights. Charles and François helped with our translation of scientific terms, theses, and formulas. Philip and Emily proofread the entire draft and Philip's help with formatting was also invaluable.

We would also like to thank EUP's Philosophy Editor, Carol Macdonald, for her indefatigable support and encouragement. Our thanks to Tristan Garcia could go without saying, but won't. We are recipients of an immense gift. And finally, we thank Speculative Realism series editor Graham Harman, both for his philosophical contributions and for his own indefatigability, tireless effort, and utter selflessness in bringing works such as this into print.

Abigail and Christopher RayAlexander
Evansville, Indiana
2017

Jon Cogburn
Baton Rouge, Louisiana
2017

For Agnes

THE LIFE INTENSE

Introduction[1]

Intensities are constantly promised to us. We are born and we grow up searching for strong sensations that might justify our lives. Whether obtained through sport, drugs, alcohol, games of chance, seduction, love, orgasm, physical joy or pain, the contemplation or creation of works of art, scientific research, fanatical faith or furious engagement, these sudden excitations awaken us from the monotony, automatism, and stammering of sameness, from existential flatness. A kind of devitalisation ceaselessly threatens comfortably settled humanity. Long ago, this numbness haunted the loafing, satisfied sovereign, the idle kings desperately seeking amusement: Nero, Caligula, or conquerors slumbering in what was referred to as 'the delights of Capua'.[2] In their triumph, a paradox threatened the superior human being; by achieving all their desires and accomplishing all their goals, they felt within themselves a relaxation of existential tension and the vigour of their nerves, and they lost that indefinable feeling that allows living beings to positively assess the intensity of their own existence.

As the economic development of the West has progressed, more and more people have enough food, shelter, and leisure time. As a result, this fear that haunts the victor has been democratised and extended to modern humans, who have become frustrated even as their needs are more satisfied. The complacent lack the feeling of truly living, which they associate with those who struggle and survive in difficult circumstances. And yet, when that feeling of nervous awareness is lost or about to be so, it is often identified as a strange internal force. Although it is impossible to quantify it precisely, that internal force is unfailingly recognised by intuition and determines the degree to which a person is engaged in their feelings. From the outside, it is always possible to evaluate whether others have what they need, if their existence is easy or difficult, and even if they are happy or unhappy. But no one can penetrate to the heart of a being in order to decide in their stead whether their manner of existence feels faint or strong. This is what cannot be taken from subjectivity: it is its inviolable fortress. There is what happens to us in the eyes of an observer, and then there is the personal measure, the internal gauge of what we experience for ourselves: that is what intensity is. Of course, we have all long been aware of the physiological signs of intensity to which our species, like all other mammals, is attentive: accelerated breathing, pounding heart, surging pulse, contraction of the arrector pili muscles, shivering, reddening of the cheeks, dilated pupils, and heightened muscle tension – the adrenaline rush. But there is also a mysterious 'degree of intensity of the self in itself' that resists being reduced to physical excitation. It is the feeling of being more or less oneself: we know all too well that the same perception, the same moment, or the same encounter can be felt more or less forcefully. The content of an experience alone does not make it intense: a seemingly insignificant instant, a gesture repeated a thousand times, or the familiar details of a face can suddenly leap out and give us a feeling of epiphany like a shock of electricity. This shock once again exposes us to the intensity of real life and pulls us out of the mire of routine which we have sunk into without even realising it. A long-awaited moment, some happy news, a terrible tragedy, or a sublime work can also sometimes leave us feeling secretly indifferent. Why? There is no exact and invariable relationship between what we experience and the intensity of our experiences. Being's erratic lightning strike allows us to momentarily attain the highest degree of our own feeling of existing. From birth to death, we develop according to the modulation of this discharge that we both hope for and dread. We try to provoke it when we lack it, and each of us tries to find a means of evaluating its amplitude and frequency. Thanks to statistics, technology promises us that it will even measure and study, if not these changes of intensity, at least their physiological effects. The recent commercialisation of internet-connected wristbands that allow individuals to monitor in real time their stress peaks, cardiac rhythm, and quality of sleep thus foster a certain type of modern person, a reader and permanent interpreter of the numerically encoded variations of their being. We are supposed to control the development of our life's intensity, which vacillates like a little roller coaster car hurtling non-stop around its track. Depending on the character and interests of each person, this frantic feeling can well up when raking in the winnings after an improbable call in poker, when winning a particularly closely fought game online, when allowing yourself a burst of speed on a deserted road, in the free fall of bungee jumping, when cliff diving or blazing a trail on a rock climb, when going hunting, when walking through the curtain with a stomach knotted in stage fright, when disregarding safety guidelines, when breaking the law, when getting together with friends to excitedly discuss rebellion, when taking to the streets to face the police, when arranging a time and a place in a car park for a fight between fans. This feeling can also well up when lying in bed reading an addictive thriller with a back cover that promises an unprecedented shock, when watching increasingly gory films, when drinking energy drinks, when snorting a line of cocaine, when masturbating, when opening yourself to chance encounters, when falling in love, or when trying to feel yourself turn back into the subject of your life, while paradoxically letting yourself go, to finally divest yourself of self-control. It might be that this all ends up assembling a sort of tool within each of us, initially rudimentary and then refined, for measuring the intensity of life, the variations of which enter into our interest calculations; we act rationally, as long as we have first regularly and more or less on demand experienced an intensity that suffices to makes us feel alive.

Western liberal society has understood this for a very long time and has directed itself towards this type of individual. Here is what we have been promised: to become intense people or, more precisely, people whose existential meaning is the intensification of all vital functions. Modern society no longer promises individuals another life, the glory of what lies beyond, but rather promises what we already are – more and better. We are living bodies, we experience pleasure and pain, we love, emotions endlessly seize us, but we also seek to satisfy our needs, we want to know ourselves and what surrounds us, and we hope to be free and to live in peace. But what we are offered is even better: the enhancement of our bodies, the intensification of our pleasures, our loves, our emotions, ever more answers to our needs, better knowledge of ourselves and the world, progress, growth, acceleration, more freedom, and a better peace. This is the very formula of all the modern promises that we are no longer totally sure we should believe: an intensification of production, consumption, communication, our perceptions, as well as our emancipation. For some centuries we have embodied a certain type of humanity: people shaped by the search, not for transcendence, as those of other epochs and cultures were, but for intensification.

At a very young age, we learn to want and desire more of the same thing. And we paradoxically learn at the same time to be on the lookout for variation and novelty. In either case, we are taught to no longer await anything absolute, eternal, or perfect. We are encouraged to dedicate ourselves to the maximisation of our entire being.

There is nothing abstract in this formula. It is rather our most concrete and most trivial condition. We only have to hear the words addressed to us daily by the merchandise we consume. In today's world, the smallest proposition of pleasure is a little promise of intensity. Advertisements are nothing but the explicit expression of this intoxication of sensation. We are sold not only the satisfaction of our needs but also the prospect both of enhanced perception and the simultaneously measurable and incalculable development of a kind of sensual pleasure. Chocolate ('86% intense'), alcohol ('intense vodka'), ice cream bars ('Magnum Intense'), flavours, and fragrances are 'intense'; this is how experiences, moments, and faces are judged.[3] By way of a more and more frequently used Anglicism, we even affirm that people are remarkable by saying that they are 'intense'. We also say it about anything strong, sudden, and original that we have consumed. One might believe that intensity therefore only pertains to the dominant vocabulary of the market-oriented world. But it's not just this. One surprising aspect of the term is that it is shared by all camps. The ideological enemies who clash in today's world have at least this ideal in common: the search for an existential intensity. Perhaps the argument for liberals, hedonists, revolutionaries, and fundamentalists really only revolves around the meaning of this existentially necessary intensity. Consumerist society and hedonistic culture sell intensities of life, but their most radical opposition also promises intensity, this time an unquantifiable intensity that's not up for sale, a supplement for the soul that the society of material goods might no longer be able to provide. Revolutionary heroism, regularly opposed to the market-oriented universe, was based on defending the intensity of 'real life' against the self-centred calculus of bodies and spirits. Poetry, song, voices of revolt, and critical discourses that sought to promote other forms of life have also reproached capitalist civilisation, the civilisation of universal calculation, for its inability to arouse an experience of the self intense enough to be desired and shared. Other 'vibrations' (hippy and rasta 'vibes') and other poetic 'guiding lights' are endlessly opposed to the illusory promises of powerful, monetised experiences. Critiques of the low existential intensity of normal Western life are common, from Rimbaud to surrealism, from Thoreau to the hippy movement, from Ivan Illich to *The Coming Insurrection*. We even regularly explain the outbreak of violent and 'deviant' behaviour, whether concerning riots or terrorism, by a mysterious defect in the soul of a consumerist society incapable of providing its youth with a sufficiently stimulating intensity of life. We imagine that the young people who leave to carry out *jihad* have turned their backs on a dismal, nondescript society that has lost its existential allure. In this way, the ideal of intensity belongs not only to the liberal world but also to its enemies. Taking intensity to be the supreme value of existence is still what we all have in common. It is our condition; it is the human condition that we perhaps inherited from modernity. Once this shared situation is laid out, those for and those against the liberal society derived from modernity contend over *what should be intense*: the satisfaction of my needs or my unconditional commitment to an idea.

But, in either case, what is this strange internal intensity of life that they promise us? The feeling that my life could not just be that of anybody whatsoever. The conviction, albeit fleeting, that I am indeed the subject of my life. After all, if I weren't assured by some *je-ne-sais-quoi* that pertains to no one else but me, another person could just as well lead my life and I could lead the life of another; everyone is replaceable. From the outside, existences can resemble each other. But what differentiates them is this internal certainty that there is a force that I alone can measure. This certainty, which is mine alone, is what others would like to reveal to me through preaching or lessons on the feeling of real life.

What is the intensity of my sensation? It's what I can never explain to others but which assures me that, for this very reason, my sensations are at least mine. This irreducible character gives intensity all of its importance. It diffuses an aura of simultaneous mystery and obviousness. By intensity, we understand the measure of that which resists measuring, the quantity of that which resists quantification, the value of that which resists evaluation. Intensity resists calculation while allowing for subjective attributions of size. Modernity entailed the rationalisation of knowledge, production, and exchange, the mathematisation of the real, and the establishment of a framework for the equivalence of all things exchangeable on a market. But intensity, as if it were a means of compensation, has come to signify the supreme ethical value of that which resists this rationalisation. Intensity is not strictly irrational, but it cannot be reduced to those figures of rationality such as objectivity, identification, division in space, number, and quantity. Little by little, intensity became the fetish of subjectivity, difference, the continuous, the countless, and pure quality.

In the domains of aesthetics, morality, and politics, intensity first served as a basis for resistance and for the expression of everything that seems singular. It signified the unique character of a feeling of intoxication or a dazzling experience, as opposed to the dividing and cutting up of the being of the world through calculating, classifying, and normative rationality. And then intensity itself became a norm, the norm for comparing each thing not in relation to other things, but *in relation to itself.* By measuring all kinds of intensities in our daily lives, we try only to evaluate the quantity of 'itself' that everything expresses. This is the guiding principle of the type of humanity that is attached to the existential value of the intense. From this point forward, what do we find most beautiful? That which intensely fulfils its being.[4] We all speak this language of intensity. People we consider beautiful are those who accept their physical features and character traits, those who do not try to be anything else, but who try to be maximally 'self-realised'.

For those of us who have accepted our inherited values from the past two or three centuries of history, this is the most profound ideal: an ideal without contents, a purely formal ideal. *To intensely be what one is.*

Thus 'aesthetic intensity' has slowly eclipsed the classical canon of beauty. In large part a fantasy of those who long for it today, this canon imagined the link between a representation and a pre-existing ideal. This ideal came to be ruled by laws of symmetry, harmony, and agreement. All these laws appeared to the modern eye like an illegitimate violence inflicted on the autonomy of image, music, or text. It was no longer a question of judging the value of a work of art according to whether or not it responded correctly to the idea of what it should be. No, it was instead hoped that a work of art might dazzle the spectator with an unprecedented experience. Think, for example, of the 'happenings', Viennese Actionism, and the Living Theatre. For the majority of disciplines, the point has become to go beyond representation through the shock of the *presence* of things. In this case, spectators seek less to savour a show than to be run through by the shuddering feeling of the uncontrollable excess of presence of what appears before them. By the same token, they manage to feel themselves a little more and feel a little more present; they tremble at the possibility of rediscovering the lost meaning of *here* and *now*. And little by little, the idea that a work should be judged in the light of its own principles took hold. Modern aesthetics consisted of bringing a work or a situation as close as possible back to its internal rules instead of external conventions. Seen from this viewpoint, nothing is totally comparable to anything else. A face, a landscape, and a movement of the body are not measured against a predetermined type of face, landscape, or movement, except by those who we would call 'neo-classical' or 'reactionary', those who still search for rules or laws of beauty. Of course, beings can be ugly, ungraceful, inharmonious, or false in view of a given cultural norm. But as we have known for a long time, these norms change. They are not everlasting. They form, expire, and perish. What is considered beautiful in one place is not in another. What is beautiful today might have been considered ugly yesterday and could be beautiful again tomorrow. With Romanticism, the West has learned or relearned how to appreciate the vulgar just as much as the beautiful. The deformed can turn into the graceful, the grotesque can become sublime. There are no absolute criteria of value bound up with the contents of a work of art. Artists can even extract magnificence from horror. They can make a sort of paradoxical jubilation or euphoria appear out of boredom, and bring forth a sort of truth from falsehood and lies.

So, how to judge? All that matters is determining if the thing is *strong*. And yet even weakness can be loved, praised, and celebrated, if it is *powerfully* weak. If mediocrity is not mediocrely rendered by a work, it finds its justification.[5] Therefore, the objective criteria of modern aesthetic sentiment prevail no longer, and now there is only a criterion focused on manner: the thing can be no-matter-what,[6] as long as it is that thing *with intensity*.

Intensity is nothing other than the principle of the systematic comparison of a thing to itself. An intense thing is more or less strongly that which it is. Be it hideous, dreadful, provocative, demanding, exciting, melancholic, depressing, audacious, gripping, disgusting, criminal, nightmarish ... nothing is a priori off limits. It does not matter what thing is considered but rather that it is, at that moment, being that thing the most and the best that it can.

And, little by little, this simple idea has oriented not just our entire aesthetic consciousness but also our ethical consciousness. Over the course of this inquiry, we will try to convince the reader that this value of intensity has become the *ethos* of our humanity. This is indeed the value that governs and orients the essentials of our conception of what we can and should be. What is a life worth? For many, particularly from the eighteenth century on, judging an existence in the light of a moral model came to be conformist and even authoritarian. The emancipation of individuals led to the modern intuition that ethics was the development by each person of their own tribunal. An existence cannot be judged in comparison with another, and a form of life cannot be forced to resemble another, since this implies the imposition of another model. However, judgements are still made about the ethical value of human life. We ceaselessly try to evaluate our own lives. But a single law presides over the modern trial of the self vs itself: that what has been done was done with a fervent heart. Clearly, there are still moral values (dignity, fidelity, respect, and so on), in accordance with which each person – following her convictions – considers the actions and the entire existence of another to be good or bad. But this *external* morality has been replaced by a sort of *internal* ethics that plunges into the heart of beings and concerns the value of a life in itself and for itself. Is it beautiful, good, wise, or foolish? Is it a happy life? Is it the life of a criminal, a saint, a shady bastard, a mean-spirited being, an ordinary person, and so on? It matters little. The only accepted principle seems to be the following: whatever the motivations and actions of a person may have been, we must finally ask ourselves if they 'lived life to the fullest', following the prosaic expression that still accurately formulates what is expected of us from now on. In everything, the only true sin is to have lacked intensity. One might have been mediocrely flamboyant, but it would have been better to have been flamboyantly mediocre.

Almost two centuries of novels, films, and songs say nothing but the following. 'Whatever you live, live!' 'Whomever you love, love!' But above all, 'Live and love as much as you can!' Because in the end nothing but this vital intensity will have counted.

And yet what seems evident to us nevertheless distinguishes us from other types of humanity who recognised as their supreme value being exalted to a sovereign state (a life after death, metempsychosis, glory, eternity) or their serene dissolution within the extinction of the variable intensities of life (illumination, nirvana, ataraxia). It seems that we belong to a type of humanity that turned away from contemplation and waiting for something absolute and, forsaking transcendence as the absolute meaning of existence, instead embraced a kind of civilisation in which the ethics of the majority latches on to the incessant fluctuation of being as its vital principle.

Maybe we are no longer capable of feeling anything but the intense, that which augments, diminishes, and varies. It might even be that this is what defines us.

Our democratic cultural life is certainly the sum total of these variable energies: the new that follows upon the new, the unprecedented and the unheard of that the modern critical mind keeps track of through the advice of magazines, blogs, and social networks, while following changes in fashion and the life of ideas and

staying away from the mundane, the habitual, and the routine . . .
Hairstyles and colours, fashion accessories, waistlines, forms and
colours of clothing, recipes, alcohol, liqueurs and cocktails, novels,
television series and songs, comedy, athletic performances, star
couples, political notions, and models of cars are all exposed to
the ebb and flow of excitation and boredom, the bolt that strikes
a person, electrifying them with novelty, and the flat encepha-
logram of a blasé individual. These tendencies, these ideological
and aesthetic waves, etch an infinite sine wave into the minds of
people, which some newspapers literally depict with highs and
lows, wins and fails, what's *in* and what's *out*, the high and the
low intensity of contemporary culture. This culture has learned to
no longer dogmatically judge using the intrinsic value of works
and ideas. Thanks to graphs of the *has been* and the 'new wave',
now everything we see around us is judged by relative force, by
climbing or falling tendencies, or by what bores and what excites.
Modern culture is indexed by this variable intensity, a sine wave
of social electricity, an approximate measurement of the degree of
individuals' collective excitation.

Of course, the cause of this excitement is important, but it's
the excitement itself that counts the most. Only this feeling of
excitement allows us to live our lives free from bitterness and
resentment. We think that a person no longer capable of excitement is lost; they are still alive but their internal life has somehow
ceased. They lead the life of the dead. They cling to old contents
of excitement that they are incapable of renewing. We pity them.

We should, therefore, admit that, generally speaking, modern life
has indeed identified some positive contents, for example, the contents of belief, the contents of commitment, and those of values,
ideas, camps, or positions. You, what do you believe in? What do you
desire? What do you judge to be just? There are moral criteria. There
are political quarrels about them. However, the norm of all norms,
on which almost everybody seems to have agreed, has imposed itself
in liberal society. It is at once very simple and difficult to grasp. It's
a superior ethical value, embodied in the cultural sine wave or the
changes in an individual's adrenaline levels, in fluctuations of desire,
pleasure, pain, convictions, truths, and styles, an uninterrupted flow
that this simple word 'intensity' designates simultaneously in our
hearts and in our minds and that orients our existence.

Intensity is the standard by which we measure the value of both our intimate life and the moment in which we live. But is it enough? Is it augmenting or is it diminishing? And this character of intensity does not just qualify fluxes or *local* cycles, it also serves to evaluate the general evolution of society. In this way, one could say that these two terms belonging to the vocabulary of intensity have acted as regulating principles in Western politics and economy ever since the eighteenth century: growth and progress. Historical progress was expressed through the struggle to reinforce certain political values: liberty and equality. The general progress of humanity was evaluated according to the intensification of this or that idea among humankind. Thanks to various indicators, from Quesnay's big 'Table' to the gross national product, from the gross domestic product to the gross national income, and from the Human Development Index to the Gini coefficient, economic growth signified the positive variation of the production of commercial goods and services. Coming and going at the whims of booms and crises, growth and progress seemed endless and incapable of completion. Neither one nor the other guided humanity towards Paradise, the City of God, or a beyond. They only served as indicators of an increase, a rational development, and hope for a perpetual improvement of the world here below. We have acted in order to vary, progress, and grow indefinitely, and this ideal appeared to us as the most just. Indeed, it seemed to be the only acceptable one. This ideal did not pretend to bring our humanity back into relation with images or definitive ideas in the heavens. Instead, it tried to adjust humanity to itself and to reinforce within humanity what was best and most human. That is, it posited that modern humanity acted on the basis of this implicit maxim: treat your own humanity and that of others in a way that always makes humanity better and more human. Intensify it. Make it advance, make it grow within you and among all others.

And yet this idea, already familiar to the modern mind, becomes intriguing once we isolate it and contemplate it from the outside. Think of a scholar in Antiquity, an intellect of the Middle Ages, a subject of the Han dynasty, or a Vedic Brahman: would they have subjected, as we do, *all their values* (aesthetic, moral, political) to this criterion of intensification? Nothing could be less certain. The absolute, eternity, truth, or simplicity would have undoubtedly won out as the final criterion of judgement. We have inherited a form of humanity that is more suspicious of these classic criteria and that has replaced them through the fetishisation of intensity. The best of what we can hope for, what we find truest and most beautiful, what we believe in, all of it returns to the intensification of what there already is. The intensification of the world, the intensification of our lives. Here we see the grand modern idea. What is certain is that neither salvation nor wisdom is to be found in this idea of intensity when we observe it from afar. It is not the promise of another life or of another world. Nor is it the perspective of equilibrium, or absolution, or self-erasure that exists in so many human cultures, internal extinction of the passions and their incessant variations. The intensity that everything in the contemporary world promises us is an ethical programme whose tiny voice whispers within all of our pleasures and all of our pains, 'I promise you more of the same thing. I promise you *more life*.'

This work will therefore endeavour to depict from the outside the condition in which our modern soul is trapped; the perspective of salvation or wisdom has been replaced by the stimulation or progress of our entire being, right up to its electrification. We will represent this intensity as the centuries-long unsurpassable horizon of our values, the secret principle of our judgements, our immense hidden a priori. Maybe this condition, this directing form of all our ideas, is already null and void. Does the simple fact that we can imagine this from the outside signal that we are halfway out of it? It is necessary to at least understand how we entered into it in the first place.

Notes

1. Following certain French literary conventions, the original text of *La Vie Intense* contains no endnotes and no bibliography. All the endnotes here, as well as the bibliography, are the translators'. We strictly follow the policy of intervening for only three reasons: 1) when Garcia is directly quoting a text, 2) when a cultural reference is likely to be missed by an interested and literate reader, and 3) when a link to *Form and Object* is worth making explicitly. Note that this still falls short of English-language conventions for endnoting!

2. The delights of Capua (*délices de Capoue*) refers to Hannibal's residence in Capua in the third century BC, where he and his soldiers enjoyed themselves for a winter and consequently lost their combative edge. In Book 23, Chapter 18 of *The History of Rome*, after describing the delights experienced by Hannibal's men ('sloth, wine, feasting, women, baths, and idle lounging'), Livy writes that 'Authorities in military matters have regarded the wintering at Capua as a greater mistake on the part of Hannibal than his not marching straight to Rome after his victory at Cannae.' The deleterious effects on the soldiers' military preparedness, as well as the beginning of the Carthaginian military reversals, are described in the beginning of Chapter 45 of Book 23.

3. While English speakers do use the word 'intense' in exactly these same ways (for example 'Whoa, that was intense, dude!'), American advertising executives have hit on the word 'extreme' to do the same work. For example, 'Doritos Extreme' are not only much better than the more pedestrian fare preferred by squares, they are also an even better version of Doritos corn chips.

4. In Book II, Chapter VIII of *Form and Object*, Garcia presents a genealogical account of the evolution of beauty that leads up to the account of beauty presupposed here, with entities being more beautiful to the extent that they are more intensely themselves. This account is explicated in Chapter 9 of Cogburn's *Garcian Meditations*.

5. This is the first use by Garcia of what becomes in Chapter 4 of this book the distinction between an adjectival notion of morality and an adverbial notion of ethics. Morality for Garcia concerns *what* entities (paradigmatically people, kinds of actions, and venerated objects) should have particular salience for how we should live our lives. Ethics is concerned with *how*, or the manner in which, we should act. For Garcia, the cultural triumph of intensity brings about the somewhat Pyrrhic victory of ethics over morality. In the above example, it doesn't really matter what your actions are, as long as you perform them intensely. This is surely a send-up of the existentialist/Heidegerrian/Sartrean cult of authenticity, which makes it striking that Garcia never mentions it in these contexts. For example, while the Sartrean view is adjectivally libertine, it is also (as perhaps all such views must be) adverbially puritanical. For such privileged views of authenticity, everything (every thing) is permitted except doing anything in an 'inauthentic' way. For the purest and hence most uncomplicated distillation of this view, see Sartre's *Existentialism is a Humanism*.

6. As discussed in the Translators' Introduction to *Form and Object* and Chapter 4 of *Garcian Meditations*, 'No-matter-what' is one of the key technical terms in *Form and Object*. What is particularly interesting (surely worth a dissertation or three) about Garcia's invocation of no-matter-what above is how he ties his own formal ontology in *Form and Object* together with the victory of the adverbial/ethics over the adjectival/morality. Since this very victory is shown to end in aporia in this book, Garcia is here hinting at the aporetic (and perhaps constitutively inconsistent) nature of his own ontological project as well as that of ontology/metaphysics proper. This theme is explored from a different angle in Cogburn's *Garcian Meditations*, but it also emerges when we apply the genealogy of Book II of *Form and Object* to the ontology found in Book I of the same work. The above quip is thus a strong hint of what is to come, both in *The Life Intense* and in the trilogy of which it is a part.

1

An Image

What Electricity Has Done to Thought

Leipzig's kiss

Where did this excitement come from?

Hawksbee built his machine,[1] and people experimented with rubbing glass balls and rods of resin. And then, during the 1740s, the phenomenon became a subject of popular wonder in the salons of Europe, especially in Germany. Fascinated by Hawksbee's experiments and Dufay's writings, Georg Mathias Bose, a young poet and physicist from Leipzig, devised a series of technical feats intended to impress a public of respectable ladies and gentlemen who hurried to admire the spectacle of this new fire, 'electric fluid', surging spontaneously from matter. What did Bose's device consist of? He would invite guests to break bread with him. Beforehand, he would insulate all the furniture and his own chair. The apprentice wizard would then discreetly touch a thin copper wire placed under a tray and connected to a hidden generator activated by an accomplice; then, with gravitas, Bose would put his hand flat on the table. The current passed along the guests' arms, which they would politely rest on this same table, and the crowd, sharing a look of panic, would become overjoyed, surprised, and dishevelled, their hair standing on end as it teemed with thousands of crackling sparks. 'It's marvellous!' one exclaimed. A few months later, Bose invented a machine for mechanical beatification, with the 'saint' seated on an insulated chair, the top of his head covered by a little pointy metal hat, under a sort of crown of bits of cardboard and junk. The current was diffused by a long wire that hung just above a metal plate. Situated barely a centimetre higher than the crown, it set off a crackling of sparks that outlined a halo above the head of the person now sanctified by science and frozen with surprise.

Bose's imagination was particularly drawn to an attraction called 'the electric kiss of Leipzig', which he lyrically describes in his poem 'Venus electrificata'. Having been insulated from the current beforehand, a beautiful young woman would be connected to Bose's primary generator, her lips coated with a conductive substance. An honourable audience member was then invited to come up and kiss the girl. The twenty-something-year-old man would bring his quivering lips close to those of the Venus and suffer a violent discharge. The astonished public would then see a surging flash between the mouths of the two young people. The man, having literally received the shock of his life, would be momentarily dazed, the power of the electricity, the fire emanating from the woman, leaving him breathless. 'The pain came from up close, and my lips were quaking. My mouth twisted, and my teeth almost broke!'

Bose, the maths professor Hausen, and Winkler, their young colleague in Eastern languages, all set Leipzig ablaze with audacious experiments straddling the line between physics and quackery; in this period, the 'electric fairy' (la fée électricité) was still a magical form of scientific entertainment, an irrational promise of reason. Soon enough, the games would be replaced by theories. But, for the time being, the fumes of this subtle fluid sparking a fire in the ether stoked the spirits of Europe and sketched the outline of a new image of human desire. 'Madame, you are now filled with fire, a fire of the purest kind, one that will cause you no pain as long as you keep it in your heart, but one which will also make you suffer as soon as you communicate it to others.' Lying latent, perhaps this internal fire is to blame for only revealing itself through contact with her suitor, the man who tries to kiss her. This fire represents the desirability of the young woman; sensual desire is like an electric force and, conversely, electricity is like the natural libido of all matter, just waiting for its suitor, humanity, to reveal itself. In the guise of desire, electricity is not without danger, but it triggers the shiver of a new intensity, that of an 'unthinkable fluid'. We still did not know the nature of this fluid or its possible uses. The human body served as the principal conductor for these first demonstrations of electrostatic power. Like an electric shiver through the body, something happens that makes manifest the occult power of certain objects to repel or attract others, to heat up, to set off sparks, and to produce a combined discharge of energy and light. But soon the human body was replaced by metal. Flesh, muscles, and nerves were separated from this mysterious impulse. It returned to its place within things, as the first electrostatic generators, Leyden jars, batteries in cylinders, and trays of thousands of jars were constructed.[2]

But then electricity entered into humanity, where it would always remain as a sort of intoxication cultivated by the modern mind. Like blood coursing through the veins of society, electric light spread through optical science and transported fabulous cinemato-graphic images to the screen. It broke the image into a thousand bits of light, decomposed and encoded it into short pulses capable of being transmitted over distances, and made way for the diffusion of television. It invaded all data, images, texts, and sounds and then placed itself in the service of electronics. It illuminated the street lights of the great capitals as well as the lamps above the beds of children reading late into the night. It fed the indefatigable motor of growth and progress. It demanded that dams, generators, power plants, and windmills be constructed. It set in motion all things or nearly all things to the extent that humanity, without even knowing it, became the living medium between entities (cables, telephones, radios, pacemakers …) Little by little, humanity forgot the electric nature of those entities, but the idea remained in the bloodstream. It was as if Leipzig's kiss, which sealed the modern alliance of desire and electricity, had never ended.

The promise of electric *Lumières*

From among the thousand possible definitions of modernity, let us take one that seems the simplest and most concrete: modernity is the domestication of electric current. The eighteenth-century emergence of an unprecedented movement towards investigation, of experiments at once erudite and lurid, and of incongruous and passionate stagings of possible applications for this new energy, made electricity, as the magical promise of reason, the central figure of modernity. Before it was the humble servant of indus-trialisation, and before it became the handmaiden of electronics and information technologies, electricity first presented itself to a curious Europe as an immense hope that left crowds weak in the knees. Electricity not only made possible the transformation of all things, but it also managed to allow for the comprehension of everything, of both nature and humanity, in the light of a new energy. Citing the work of Daniel Roche, André Guillerme summarises it well:

> Electricity is, in the last third of the 18th Century, more than a popular science, more than a new science of physics and medicine, a social science of the *Lumières*. At once mechanical, chemical, military, biological, physical, pharmacological, philosophical, meteorological, and economical (wasn't it Galvani's ambition to discover the motor of the animal's economy in its nerves?), even mineralogical and agronomical, it runs through all domains of knowledge and galvanises the public forum; it forwards a new image of humanity and plays the role of a 'perceptible revelator of all those movements' that bewilder Western society.[3]

The French revolutionary Barbaroux dedicated the following emphatic verses to this new 'revelator', 'O subtle fire, soul of the world, beneficent electricity / You fill the air, the earth, the sea, the sky, and its immensity.'[4] A century later, in his painting *The Electricity Fairy*, Dufy rediscovered the vibrant hues and naïve accents of the minds that lauded the incredible discovery of electricity and saw in it the driving energy of modernity, liberating humanity from antediluvian drudgery (brushing, washing, heating, cooking …), and allowing for upgrades and refinements of vision or hearing and replacements or accentuations of the human body's natural energy. For several centuries, modern times were the expression of a collective movement of enthusiasm that united confidence in progress, the hope for a definitive emancipation of humanity, and faith in technology within the project of knowing the totality of humanity and the world from a fistful of verifiable principles. The fascination with electricity was the first driving force of this enthusiasm. Electricity reconciles theory and practice; it both acts and explains at once. In a 1786 essay, the Count of Tressan saw in electric fluid what he called a 'universal agent', and, four years later, Roucher-Deratte raised it to the rank of a principle of life, contending that the electric fluid of the animal is the observable, scientific analogue of the soul as understood by the metaphysicians. He claimed this to be composed of equal parts electricity and animal gas. This fluid gives shape to the life force and, consequently, the libido; one of the characters from Madame de Morency's novel *Illyrine* doesn't know how to resist the 'electric hand' of desire. This impalpable erotic energy thus takes on a physical form. But the Prince of Ligne and the Count of Maistre also explained both military discipline and wartime rivalries in terms of electrification. Chénier summed up the enthusiasm of an auditorium in terms of 'theatrical electricity'. As for Sade, he used electrical vocabulary with the aim of redefining the very terms of morality. At the end of the eighteenth century, Snetlage's dictionary of neologisms noted that the adjective 'electric', which was only used to describe observable bodies, had been generalised to the movements and tremors of the soul itself, and proposed the following sentence by way of illustration: 'The electric fire that inflames the hearts of all the soldiers of liberty.'

As Michel Delon showed in *L'Idée d'énergie au tournant des Lumières* (1988), attention to the electric phenomenon allows for a rethinking of *enlightenment* in its literal sense, as a type of Illuminism. Just like the spectators at Leipzig's experiments with the *Venus electrificata*, modern Europe had been permeated by a shock, a desire, and a formidable promise of illumination. Streets, houses, and factories, but also hearts and consciousness would be set alight thanks to the energy of storms, which had previously been thought to be reserved for Jupiter, the master of the thunderbolt. And humanity would steal fire from the gods a second time; this time, the fire would be electric fluid.

The same fluid courses through amber, storms, and our own nerves

We know all too well what material civilisation owes to electricity, but we do not often ask ourselves what electricity has done to thought and morality.

Its most important effect may not be the most evident. Electricity holds the fleeting promise of reunifying our fields of knowledge.

Matter, life, and thought, all equally permeated by the electric current, could be newly conceived of as moments of a continuity, and not as a succession of absolutely distinct states or domains. It had long been known that inorganic nature is filled to bursting with electricity, and amber and lightning were the visible symptoms of this fact, but we also found that every sensible body had nerves and that information regarding sensibility, pain, and pleasure was communicated within an organism through the circulation of this same subtle fluid – electricity – that sprang forth at the moment when amber was rubbed and when storms began to rage. Extrapolating from La Caze's works, the *Encyclopédie* article on 'Generation' discusses the hypothesis of a hidden 'electric matter' at work in the male's semen and the female's womb. In his research on the physics of electricity, Marat reckoned that this electric power is the 'general agent' of nature. It's the force that traverses nature, sets it in motion, and permeates all that vibrates, suffers, and feels.

To live was therefore to be electric.

In the 1780s, Bertholon evoked the idea of an 'animal electricity' and a 'human electricity', but it was the Italian scholar Galvani's pamphlet *De viribus electrictatis in motu musculari commentarius*, published in 1791, through which the revolutionary hypothesis of an electric nature causing muscular and nervous movements in animal organisms was disseminated throughout all of learned Europe (a considerable editorial feat at that time). Rather than resorting to the generally accepted hypothesis of animal spirits, notably formulated by Haller and the Hallerists, who were still studying 'physiological irritability', Galvani used frogs and pigs to overturn the old notions, replacing them with the new concept of electricity.

The idea of electricity as a vital force could not stand up to analysis for long. Though a convert of galvanism, Volta wondered if a frog were not simply a sort of Leyden jar and if the electricity artificially produced by a capacitor and the muscular and nervous electricity produced by an animal could be added and subtracted. His research soon brought him to defend the electromotive powers of metal against Galvani. The development of his battery, which opened the path to a new source of energy – namely, the chemical energy produced by contact between metals – lent solid credibility to the followers of Volta. As he understood it, electricity is a phenomenon of the inorganic world which, while undoubtedly in contact with the living, is not the principal factor for sensate organisms. Rather than being the essence of life, electricity is an energy shared by the organic and the inorganic alike. This is much like what we think today: electricity certainly has nothing to do with a vital force. And yet, supplementing the shortcomings of esoteric mesmerism, galvanism established a phantasmatic concept in the European mind, that of a biological electricity. Who knows? In this way there might have been hope for a new harmony between matter and life.

Animal electricity, or animal magnetism, which is to say the discovery of the electric nature of that which runs through the nerves of sensate organisms all the way through to their brains, will have served as a Trojan horse for intensity in life and thought. Inasmuch as it is sensitive, life is nervous, and inasmuch as it is nervous, life is electric. As for thought, because it is cerebral, it too is nervous, meaning that thought is electric as well. We would soon learn to measure the difference of electrical potential on the surface of the human skull, for the first time offering access to a representation of cerebral activity through the intermediary of the electroencephalogram.

Beyond merely shaping the modern development of techniques, modes of production, and reproduction, the captivating discovery of electricity also revealed thought, that most abstract of entities, to in fact have something in common with sensate life. It also revealed that the nature of sensate life had something in common with insensate matter. A phantasm as much as a reality, 'electricity' was the name of the natural current that at once explained magnetism, sensate life, and the concrete function of the mind by way of the flow of a fluid or natural fire.

Measuring the current

Electric current was first imagined as an occult fluid partly hidden from human perception. It was a sort of living river, intangible and invisible, one secretly flowing through the heart of matter and life. Electricity only revealed its latent qualities, its force, and its compelling power if we were able to divert it to our advantage thanks to experimental devices – just as primitive humanity had learned to benefit from the movement of water.

For a long time flowing water served as the ultimate representation of the future. All things moved like the river, that incessant flow that could not be held back by hand. It's Heraclitus' river ('No man ever steps into the same river twice').[5] It's Lao Tzu's river that always finishes up carrying away the enemy. It's also the raging path of a storm that Machiavelli compared to fortune, which can be rerouted by a dam but quickly bypasses it. It's the motif of a waterfall opposed to an impassable boulder in the first classical Chinese painting of the Song dynasty.

For humanity, of all visible things, flowing water still best indicated impermanence, the passing of time, and at the same time the power of becoming. This power arose from water's ability to take on all forms and, because of its fluidity, to vanquish nearly every kind of resistance.

Since electricity could only be perceived through certain of its spectacular effects, water was often used as an analogy for it. Electricity became a sort of invisible water, nestled in the very heart of matter, and was initially called a 'subtle fluid'. Hence, it was water made of fire that mixed the qualities of the first (movement and fluidity) with those of the second (heat and light) to form an unprecedented energy. And since the image of flowing water represented the future and perpetual change, electric current also picked up this connotation, and it became the new emblem of a universal future without people even realising it. It did so indirectly, by way of one of its first measurable qualities, which emerged from comparison with the water of rivers: intensity.

We know that, ever since the first years of interest in magnetism, it was the 'mother science' of hydrology that acted as a model for the conception and measurement of imponderable fluids and semi-fluids. Unlike water, electricity was the flow of something quasi-invisible, but its behaviour was still similar to that of water. So, as in hydrology, we investigated the conservation of this wave's energy. We also investigated its idiosyncratic effects, meaning the conduction or resistance to this flow according to its environment. By measuring charge, thrust, energy expenditure or output, potential energy, and the polarities and tensions of this current, we conserved the hydraulic metaphor. Apparently there was little difference between what we decided to call 'electric intensity' and the current of a river. Just as the difference in height between the highest and lowest points of a water's course on a stretch of equal width and depth allows us to calculate the quantity of water flowing through an imaginary section at the bottom of the slope, so the difference in charge between the two ends of a circuit allows us to calculate the quantity of positive or negative charge circulating at a given place and time. If we take the example of a section of electrical wire, we can see how we conventionally define the rate of flow of electrical charge across a given surface. The intensity of the current, measured in amps (amperes), is equal to a delta (δ) of electrical charge divided by a delta of time. Furthermore, we know that an amp corresponds to a rate of flow of charge of one coulomb per second, which is to say, the passage through a given point of $6.24150962915265 \times 10^{18}$ elementary charges during a single second.

By 'intensity' we therefore now mean a double difference, a difference in charge within a difference in time. Thus, intensity is only within time; all intensity is a variation between two instants. Intensity is not instantaneous. This definition also indicates that what temporal variation measures is itself a second variation, the variation of an occult quality of matter not directly accessible to human perception – its charge. No longer just meaning a shock or a blazing natural flash, electrical intensity now designates the quantifiable measurement of that flash.

The image of an idea

The discovery and exploration of the electric phenomenon had charged the matter of dreams and images with something irreducibly intense, something inscribed directly into the things themselves, an energy inherent in matter, an energy that might turn out to be the universal agent of life. But this idea of a pure intensity, glimpsed upon the revelation of electrical current during the first electrical experiments of the eighteenth century, quickly gave way to a science that exactly measured electric current. This reduced its magical power to a quantifiable expenditure of particles during a given period of time.

Electric current did not live up to the promise that it might at once explain everything and remain itself inexplicable. Once explained in terms of quantities, analysed, and broken down, it gained in physical reality what it had lost as a metaphysical idea.

The idea of electricity as the universal agent of nature, as the principle capable of explaining life and what was to come, and as the essential motor of all that lives, feels, and suffers, was (like every idea of a metaphysical energetic principle meant to explain the world) destined to disappoint when translated into the material world. Like *qì*, *prāna*, the breath of life, the *pneuma*, and like all the souls in the world, the subtle fluid of electricity failed to survive both as a metaphysical idea and as a physical entity. By fully becoming the latter, it was forced to cease being the former. Because the reduction of the intensity of electric currents to a measurable size proved highly useful, the intensity of electric currents almost immediately stopped representing the promise of a re-enchantment of the world and the principle of unity in nature, a magical reunification of what is, lives, and thinks.

Electricity's promises – not as a source of energy but as the idea reconfiguring all we knew about nature and humanity – were very fragile in theoretical form. They were essentially used as popular or scholarly representations or as very imprecise impressions, like the sort of childish and feverish experience of the public viewing the *Venus electrificata* experiment. We were happy to be transported by a physical phenomenon in the guise of a magic trick, an illusionist's trick performed by nature itself.

Understood as a pure intensity, electricity was not just an idea at first, it was an image, the image of a charge, a knowable nature that could be domesticated, but that was still animated by something wild, irreducible, and full of electromagnetic force. It signalled a difference of potential inscribed in the very elements of the physical world. There was something of a pure quality in charged matter, a sort of savage quality, and yet the intensity that resulted was not beyond calculation: we could observe and evaluate it. Below what the human senses perceived of the natural world, there subsisted an intensive material reality that captured imagination. Even better, the electrical intensity that travelled through certain portions of material also came to define sensibility, the nervosity of living things. Better still, this intensity passed through the brain, meaning that it moved within thought as well. Nature was not dead! It lived by a violent code that modern humanity could admire, just as the first humans were hypnotised by the mystery of the same fire that they hoped to domesticate.

After the project to rationalise movement and matter, this vague image excited Europe and got the modern project going because it made the world not only thinkable and knowable, but also liveable. Without intensity, the world could be reasonably considered, but when it came to living, it appeared only as a general depression of being, the result of the long history of European metaphysical and physical rationalisation of space, movement, matter, and the energy of all things. From out of this universal calculation there came the dazzling and fantastical image of an electric current, and its much sought-after intensity became the saviour of the modern spirit that had been so threatened by reason's stagnation. Electricity was the evidence of a power suppressed both in nature and our nature. It was at once domesticable and indomitable, and although it was identifiable it was also always different. It was intense.

Notes

1. In 1705 Francis Hawksbee (Francis Hauksbee the Elder) discovered that mercury stored in a vacuum emitted a glow when the ball encasing it was rubbed. This machine was the first of many that he developed to explore the properties of electricity and was also the progenitor of gas discharge, neon, and mercury vapour lamps.
2. We owe thanks to Charles Pence for his help with translating the scientific terminology throughout, and in particular the term 'plateaux aux mille bouteilles', or 'trays of thousands of jars' here.
3. Guillerme, 'L'électricité dans ses premiers grandeurs (1760–1820)', p. 6.
4. Darnton, *Mesmerism and the End of the Enlightenment in France*, p. 29.
5. Plato, *Cratylus*, 402a.

2

An Idea[1]

To Compare a Thing with Itself

Thanks to potential[2]

While strolling along, I see the day's first rays of dawn break through. All is radiant. A few minutes before, the dark hues of the landscape had already changed. In the half-light, rather than taking on a different colour, the more or less distinct forms had instead revealed more precise shades of the same; the greys, the ochres, and the greens themselves appeared more piercing and pronounced. Soon, without my being able to say precisely when the daily metamorphosis began, light spread from the horizon over the plains; even the air itself seemed to shine with greater and greater brilliance. The animals' noises and above all the birds' songs also resonated with growing strength. Nothing new appeared, yet everything seemed transfigured; all around me, the same world presented itself to me under a more intense light. I can certainly picture the successive states of the surrounding countryside in order of their degrees of brightness, but alas! By reconstituting the scene, I thereby lose the sense of becoming and continuity that made them more than merely several landscapes succeeding one another. I lose that which allowed the very same landscape to gain brightness without becoming another landscape. I can just as well imagine one and the same landscape as moving, one single image from the beginning of the sequence to the end. But it is futile. I can no longer manage to compare the almost entirely black land of the beginning and the vivid, radiant land of scarcely a few minutes later. To measure their difference, I have to distinguish them.

The same goes for all that presents itself to me as a variation. Subjected to persistent, throbbing headaches, the force of which continues to increase, I clearly *feel* the intensity of this pain, but I struggle to *think* about it. Why? If I try to measure the supplementary suffering that has gnawed at me ever since waking up, I must, through an operation of mental subtraction, imagine my current pain and remove from it my earlier pain. The remainder obtained equals the degree of supplementary pain that I gained during the interval. To do this, I have to separate out the two pains and compare them externally, in the same way that one might compare a taller man with a shorter man. From that moment on, I can no longer manage to think the intensity of my suffering, there being no variation of intensity between two elements that are exterior to one another. I can only think their difference in terms of extension. One pain is stronger than the other, just as one person is taller than his neighbour or one section of space is more extended than another. If, on the other hand, I refuse to divide up my suffering, I find myself incapable of thinking the difference in intensity that I wanted to evaluate. If my suffering is the same from early morning up to now, then I cannot say that it was stronger here or weaker there. My suffering remains identical.

This thought might seem enigmatic. Why forward a litany of concepts for something that continually and clearly imposes itself on my perception? I don't need to know it, I feel it. The thing is varying, changing, becoming. However, one of the most important and most difficult tasks of a thinking being is just this, to put into words the comparison of a thing, not with another, but *with this thing itself*. The primordial experience of a living body that feels changes consists of an incalculable series of minuscule operations that, through the intermediary of our memory, ceaselessly relate an entity back to what it was. To us the entity appears a little bit taller, a little less thick, and, in any case, different from what it was. It happens thus for the child who has grown since the last time we saw him, for blossoming love, for the rising sea level, for the tree we cut at winter's end. But the qualities of these things also fluctuate, the luminosity lowers, the cold prevails, and the sounds of merrymaking grow quiet. And as I speak, I have to be able to think what I perceive and put this modulation into words.

And yet, *potential* was first conceived in traditional Western thought in terms of the variation of the same. As defined by Aristotle, the Greek *dynamis* began as an extraordinary means of comparing each thing with itself.

The bud and the child are what they are, but they are also potentially what they will become. In this way potential, the Greek *dynamis*, served for centuries as the cardinal tool with which Western philosophy achieved the aim of relating a subject back unto itself. That potential can be summed up as a form injected into the very heart of things, the 'internal gradient' of all that is. Since every thing contained in itself the idea of its realisation (its completion in actuality), Greek, and later Christian, thought was equipped with a measuring instrument that made it possible to use understanding and perception to compare what a thing is right there – right there in front of me – with the perfect form that it ideally carries within and which might become actual. Ahead of time, I could perceive in the block of marble everything that the stone could become – including the most beautiful of statues. I could sense the blossoming flower in the bud as well as the mature man in the child. In this way, it is possible to mentally situate each of the world's singular entities so that they are accompanied by a sort of interior scale determining an achievement level with respect to their *eidos* (that is, their ideal form).

We know well the degree to which Aristotle's cosmology permitted the eye and the human mind to master intensities, whether physical or spiritual, which means ordering the chaos around and within us according to the *more* or *less* of the potential of each thing.

Since every natural being contained within it such an ideal yardstick, nothing was ever alone with itself. Year after year, in order to find my way in my own existence, I myself have occasionally situated myself on some intimate scale, enclosed within my being. At every moment, I occupy an intermediary degree on this scale, with a maximal degree indicating my full realisation in actuality. Potential was understood as the gradation of intensities of the self that each thing carried within it like its most essential identity. Under the influence of Aristotle and up to the Classical Age, beings were thus charged with an incredible interior intensity. The tree, the person, and the statue all held in the depths of their being their idea, their maximal degree of realisation. Through thought, each thing could be compared to its maximal state of completion. Thinking was nothing other than ceaselessly measuring the distance separating the actual thing from the ideal, perfected thing.

More or less

However, it is not enough to consider the progress of every natural being with respect to its idea. Evaluating each substance's degree of perfection is a problem; the measurement of the simple variation of this substance's qualities also measures something else; the brightness and whiteness of a surface can ceaselessly increase or decrease. I can perceive the modulations, but how can I *think* them?

The process whereby light becomes more or less strong or clear does not exactly seem to be extensive. By 'extensive', we mean a relation of comparison between distinct things, inasmuch as this relation is purely exterior. A quantity of matter or space is added to the smallest thing, just as 4 is joined to 1 to make 5. Yet intensity, which is never named as such by Aristotle and remains vague until the Middle Ages, represents a strange challenge for thought. It is an entirely familiar figure of change that nonetheless supposes a *non-extensive* change of qualities. It is something that, while changing, neither expands nor shrinks nor becomes something else. It is something to which nothing from outside is added, but which appears to grow or diminish from within, all the while persisting in being what it is. It's the same light that is more or less bright. In the Aristotelian texts, the affections of bodies (heat or light) and the affections of the soul (greater or lesser anger or desire in a spirit) matter equally. Aristotle repeatedly asked himself what allowed us to measure such a variation, such a *more* or *less*, in a way that did not presuppose piece by piece addition, extrinsic diminution, or augmentation. How, then, can we compare a quality with itself, and how can we find it at once identical and 'more or less what it is'?

When the wall becomes increasingly white; when the landscape becomes increasingly bright; when, to tell the truth, I become more and more annoyed, neither the wall, the landscape, nor myself

change. Being's support, or substance, is not susceptible to qualitative variation. But on substance, this invariable coat hanger of
being, are hung certain qualities that come and go, qualities such as
colour, weight, temperature, or passions.

To understand how something becomes more or less hot,
bright, just, or hard is to account for the way that qualities undergo
'intensification' (augmentation) or 'remission' (diminution) and to
take up again Aristotle's reflection in *Categories*, 'Again, a thing is
called more, or less, such-and-such than itself; for example, the
body that is pale is called more pale now than before ...'[3] For
Aristotle, intensification and remission were undoubtedly a limited sort of alteration, one that did not change the species of the
object. By 'alteration', he normally meant a change such that the
thing became another thing. Yet in the cases that interest us here, it
is evident that the thing stays the same while the intensity of one
of its qualities grows or diminishes. It is at once an identical and a
changing thing.

It seems that Aristotle resolved this paradox by again using the
categories of potentiality and actuality. The variation of a quality's
intensity corresponds to an inverse function: the more the contrary
of the quality *is* potentially, the more the quality itself *is* actually. In
other words, while the darkness of the wall is less and less real, but
also more and more possible, the brightness of the wall becomes
more and more real and less and less possible. Potential was thus the
principle of explanation not just for the varying perfections of all
natural beings, but also for the varying intensities of their qualities.
Much of Greek, Latin, Christian, and Arabo-Islamic knowledge
rested on this idea, which made it possible to treat identity and
change in a rationalistic manner.

And then this principle no longer seemed satisfactory.

The history of what we call the 'latitude of forms' allows us to
understand how, in medieval philosophy, the problem of the *inten-
sio* and *remissio* of qualities led to the progressive abandonment of
explanation of change through potential, and the favouring of *measure* of change through quantities, extensive magnitudes. In the West,
belief in the idea of potential was abandoned little by little. It seems
that the question of 'more or less' handed down by Aristotle first
offered several solutions in an attempt to accommodate potential

and measure. All of those solutions were conceived in a way that reduced intensity of potential to extension.

Indeed, the flaw of all metaphysical explanations through potential is that they do not allow for variation to be quantified. Yet as it became increasingly important for European sciences to be able to quantify movement, it became necessary to think that variations of light, sound, and all kinds of other qualities were not just tied to the metaphysical interplay of the potential and the actual. Instead, the variations of those qualities would now be explained in terms of a measurable physical change. Diminishing light and increasing noise could be measured. For this reason, medieval philosophers subjected Aristotle's strictly qualitative conception of variation to an increasingly quantitative interpretation, until the quantification of quantities and movement was complete. This made way for Descartes' notion of matter as a pure extension and the formation of Newtonian physics.

The medieval problem often consisted of asking about the intensification or remission of charity, and therefore of love, in the human soul. From an Aristotelian point of view, when I love more, it is not that a little love is added to the love I already have. The overall quality remains unchanged. Only the internal relation between the intensification and remission of love is at stake in this power dynamic. And yet this conception forbids measuring the degree of love at each instant because I finish up in a vicious circle. To determine the quantity of love in my heart at instant t is nothing other than to define the corresponding quantity of non-love; to define the one is to define the other. In the absence of an external standard, it is impossible to measure what is augmented or diminished. To do this, we must admit, as did the medieval interpreters of Aristotle, that qualities are not completely determined beings, that they allow for a measurable 'latitude' of addition or subtraction of themselves, and all of that without becoming something else entirely. The brightness of day is such that I can subtract a small quantity of it without it ceasing to be bright. Such an idea certainly supposes that a quality can be separated into small quantifiable parts. There exist, then, degrees of joy and suffering, just as there are degrees of whiteness; this idea of an 'intensive quantity' or an 'intensive magnitude' is the key to comprehending the reasoning through which the sciences of nature approached change, by which I mean the comparison of the self to the self.

Beginning in the Middle Ages, we can detect a long philosophical hesitation regarding the terms of this reasoning. For example, according to the notions of Godefroid de Fontaines or Walter Burley, every quality that varies integrally renews itself. From second to second, the landscape that I contemplate as it sinks into darkness repeatedly becomes one completely different landscape after the other. Each time it is every bit a landscape under a certain degree of luminosity. The following instant, although appearing to be a new landscape of the same type, it is actually a completely new landscape, darker, harbouring a stronger predisposition towards darkness. And if I feel more and more joy in my heart, it means that my heart is annihilated instant by instant and replaced by a totally different heart, one whose joy is more perfect.

But then the identity of what varies becomes very problematic. Since we must be able to cut time into an infinite succession of instants, there exists an infinity of versions of the same thing, each one subject to a different intensity. We lose the benefit of intensity as a measure for comparing a thing with itself. Each degree corresponds to a distinct thing.

This is why, according to the additionalist concept of the Franciscans and the Oxford Calculators, intensification is understood as a partial addition of a quality, and not a complete renewal. If I feel less sad, it means that a small part of my sadness has disappeared. The quality is thereby treated like a quantity. Sadness, joy, whiteness, brightness, and scent are no longer considered to be indivisible forms. Instead they are taken to be results of the part by part processes of construction and destruction that are the object of measure and calculation.

It is no longer a question of internal potential. On the whole, all that varies can be reduced, all in all, to some quantity, or in any case, to a homogeneous space that can be chopped up bit by bit in order to make comparison and measurement possible. In this case, we are contemplating a world no longer composed of distinct substances, each one of them brimming over with potential. This is a world in which their qualities are no longer subject to variation stemming from the occult power dynamic between a quality and its contrary. We observe a rational world where everything is equally extended, divisible, and ready to be subjected to a universal force.

Thanks to force

The classical age of the sciences is in the first instance the moment of the reduction of all intensity to nothingness. In preparing the conception of general Newtonian mechanics, classical thought identified objectivity with the absence of intensity and, therefore, identified it with extension. There was no 'more or less' interior of things. The Cartesian *res extensa*, a simple support for geometric transformations, well represents the hope of thinking a homogeneous, undifferentiated matter, one not constituted of singular substances, each the bearer of potential. Instead, the *res extensa* was an immense paste, both extensive and malleable, like an impotent gruel devoid of ideas. The impersonal matter that offered itself to modern science was the same in each of its points, with the parts adding themselves to one another externally, through combination or subtraction. Nothing in matter contained variable intensities, in the sense that nothing in nature is *more* or *less* what it is.

This was first the object of classical science, and then of modern science, an equally divided being that is, in principle, *equally* what it is. No part of the world exists better or more perfectly than another; each part can be measured externally, we can determine its size and mass, and it can be subjected to variations of force. But each part, in itself, is just like any other part of nature, an anonymous parcel without any particularity whatsoever.

The Newtonian decision is clearly articulated in the *Principia*: 'The qualities of bodies, which admit neither intension nor remission of degrees, and which are found to belong to all bodies within the reach of our experiments, are to be esteemed the universal qualities of all bodies whatsoever.'[4]

While potential was an interior *more* or *less* that inhabited and haunted each of the world's entities, force, the scientific sense of which is set by Newton even though there is no strict definition in the *Principia* (it is a primitive term that remains undefined, while making it possible for other terms to be defined), receives all the intensity expelled from matter and imprisoned in the impersonal action of what puts bodies in motion. Let us summarise it in this way: the classical age splits being into one part that is passive and absolutely not intense (matter or bodies) and one part that is intense but inconsistent (force). What is moved has no intensity, but what moves varies and is therefore intense. What is moved is a body; what moves has no body. *Force is thus an intensity of nothing exerted on everything.*

One of the most important and often discussed gestures of Newton's *Principia* takes place during the formulation of the conditions for induction, where the decision is made to refuse to give an account of the qualities of things that increase or decrease by degrees. In order to provide a rationalist account of motion, classical mechanics initially jettisons variations of luminosity, heat, sound, and odour. Those things no longer pertain to the privileged domain of what can be measured and calculated with reason.

What is Newton's force? Or, we might ask, what is force for Newton? One could say it is the potential of singular things uprooted from their specific form, from their interiority, and from their hidden essence. That potential is then projected outwards and attributed *en bloc* to the extended and impersonal matter of the world. For every separated substance there is a potential; such was the ancient cosmos, and it had begun to seem archaic. With classical physics, there is but one single potential, which, rather than being lodged in the heart of each entity, exists as a principle exterior to things and blindly and equally impresses itself on to all things from without. Contrary to Aristotelian potential, which expressed the form of each entity, force understood by Newton no longer pays any heed to what constitutes an object's identity. Newtonian force instead fleshes out a milieu of constraint that is indifferent to the entities on which it acts; it is exerted, neither more nor less, upon an equal mass and similar form, be it oak or beech, wood or lead, metal or skin. In the person who falls, the horse propelled forward in its course, the blustering of the wind, or the rock that rolls along the slope, it is always the same universal force.

In truth, Newton defined two distinct forces, or two aspects of the same force: one force from within, the force of inertia, matter's resistance to whatever imprints and constricts it; and a force from outside, which is pressure, properly speaking the shock produced by one body on another in accordance with Newton's Third Law (for every action, there is an equal and opposite reaction). 'Inertial force' and 'impressed force' are the adret and ubac slopes of the same mountain range, this immense force for which no definition exists.[5]

Breaking with the metaphysical character of Aristotelian *dynamis*, stoic *pneuma*, and primordial energy concepts expressed in terms of *qì*, *prāṇa*, and *soma*, force no longer purports to be a metaphysical principle, but merely a physical one. However, it remains a principle because it is the subject of a circular definition. To explain what force is, it must be presupposed.

This a priori use of the concept of force initially convinced Newton's English disciples. However, with the spread of the project of the rationalisation of the mechanical, it quickly became untenable. Truesdell notes that 'the notion of force is the weakness of Newton's treatment that Mach, following Leibniz and d'Alembert, saw fairly clearly'.[6] Some fifty years after the publication of the *Principia*, d'Alembert was already hoping to reduce force to a simple manifestation of movement. He evoked the forces at work in Newton as so many 'obscure and metaphysical beings which are only capable of spreading shadows on a science clear in itself'.[7] In the eyes of the most materialistically inclined, force was just as embarrassing as ether was for classical physics. Either the indefinable concept of force had to be analysed in terms that could be shown to be reasonable, or else it had to be expelled from the domain of science. Following in the footsteps of d'Alembert, both Kirchoff and Mach tried to reformulate the Newtonian project of general mechanics by limiting the need to resort to the concept of force – but without ever convincing the scientific community.

At the 1900 Paris International Conference, Poincaré summed up two centuries of questions by publicly wondering if the equation $F = ma$ was experimentally verifiable insofar as 'we still do not know what mass and force are'.[8] In Dransfeld's recent physics textbook,[9] we still read that force 'is not subject to definition'. Force is the cause of acceleration. As such, it is certainly the cause of something real, observable, and quantifiable. From this, we deduce that force is also real. However, no proof of it exists.

It is impossible to provide a rationalistic account of force, but also impossible to do without it.

In the Newtonian system that a knowledgeable Europe inherited from the eighteenth century, force is the only real intensity. Everything is what it is, no more, no less; only force varies. This will be the key formula of classical rationalism. Nothing varies in itself, and neither the apple nor I myself are more or less what we are. All of the variation in being is thus physically explained by the exercise of some force.

Fundamentally, European rationalism is this great split – all of the identity goes to entities, and all of the intensity goes to force. Force is only variation, and the things of the world do not themselves undergo modulations of being. No person is more or less a person. No blade of grass is more or less the blade of grass that it is. To think otherwise is to claim to measure the incommensurable, a change of being in itself.

With respect to itself, force is *nothing but* variation. It is *nothing but* more or less. It therefore has no identity, and the price to pay for this device is that force is not an entity. It is not incarnate, and it is not one of those things of the world on which it exerts itself. Force is a phantom. It's an intangible and indefinable intensity. What is tangible and definable admits no variation in the intensity of its being. Consequently, the universal variation of intensity that is force is neither tangible nor definable.

This is the destiny of rationalism. Inasmuch as everything is explained, the very principle of explanation escapes from the domain of the explicable, just as the source of illumination, in lighting a whole room, may itself remain in darkness. We can account for all things except for the way in which we account for all things. That is the meaning of the modern concept of force, an instrument of mechanical rationalisation *par excellence* that remains desperately opaque to the sort of elucidation that its usage otherwise makes possible.[10]

By explicating everything in terms of forces, science fails more and more to account for precisely what force itself is.

Post-Newtonian depression

Gone was the euphoric moment sparked by the Newtonian project, and a certain sort of secret fear had come to light. This fear was communicated to thought down through the centuries before getting mixed up with all the critiques of modernity, the anxiety of a depression of reason, a deprivation of intensity. By 'depression', we mean both the psychological sense and the first, literal sense of the word, a deflation of being that collapses like a soufflé due to theoretical bubbles of premodern illusions. Everything ends up looking like what it truly is, flat.

In the absence of an idea of intensity, the rationalistic account of the world made it impossible for European thought to consider the fact that something is more or less than it is as anything but irrational. It eludes calculating reason's power to consider the measure of a being *with relation to itself.* After all, the mountain is a mountain. It is the mountain that it is. We can neither praise it for being particularly well, nor blame it for being too feebly.[11] When its colours turn at dawn, I can objectively analyse this variation on the light spectrum and measure it in terms of amplitude of frequency. I can likewise reduce the appearance of an intensive variation to a series of decipherable states.

Every variation of the intensity of a being must therefore either be cut up and explained in terms of extension or raised up from out of the subject that perceives it. Pure intensity is not of this world, it is nothing more than the *sentiment* of the world. I am tired, and everything seems to drag on; I am drowsy, and everything appears in a paler light. The same world that appears lively to a person burning with desire seems bleak to a person jaded by existence. But the world is not in itself lively or bleak. What is it then? It is extended. It occupies space and time. But it has no intensity. None of its parts is worth more than any other. No piece of this world has an ontological dignity superior to that of any other piece. A volume of marble is equivalent to the size of the same volume of decomposing matter. A square centimetre of the most beautiful woman's skin equals the surface area of a square centimetre of a leper's epidermis. A dead body is no more than a living body that occupies a comparable amount of space. To those entering modernity, being had no degrees. Or it could be that, as soon as it appears to me that there are degrees, this gradation all comes down to me.

Since it happens frequently, let's say that the world seems less vivid and more sombre to me as I grow older and youth recedes. I can admit that the world itself is neither more nor less lively than before and that its variation is bound up with the state of my soul and nothing more. But then all intensity is expelled from the world and shut up within myself, making me its sole depository. Things in themselves have no intensity, they are nothing other than what they are. I add some variation of tone or vividness that reflects my psychological or physiological state. On the outside, all things are extended and measurable part by part. The feeling that the external world is more or less intensely coloured by these shifting shades, by this humour, is mine alone.

For the modern spirit, recognising the truth comes down to mourning the passing of an objective intensity of things and admitting that there are only intensities in the impressions of living beings, and that this is particularly the case with human beings. But taken objectively, and no longer subjectively, each part of this world is what it is, neither more nor less than any other. And nothing is more or less what it is. The only thing that really varies is the force exerted.

And now the first symptom of the modern conscience's depression appears: the subject can only turn within itself in its search for something intense. The truth is that outside of itself, nothing is better and nothing is worse. All is equal. Of course, force is there to explain movement and change, but it is a blind and impersonal force. Varying, but intangible, force is impossible to subject to direct experimentation.

Western culture inherited a world made both of matter without intensity and of a universal force that exerts itself from without. Western culture then felt an absence that was cruel and almost impossible to define because this force could only be felt through its effects.

This vague feeling haunted modern rationalism, that the world had become unlivable, or more exactly, it offered no sufficiently stimulating reason for living it, inhabiting it, or experimenting on it. Faced with a near-complete conversion of the world into extension, the world thus understood remained incapable of offering a vibrant, exciting image of reality to the imagination.

The idea of an image

Precisely because it appeared to save the modern European subject from this stagnation, electricity worked as a new image for the intensity within things that rationalism no longer allowed people to conceive of as a part of the world.

At present, we understand better the fascination with electricity that shook up the European public. This was the price of modernity, consciously or unconsciously; magnetism and then electricity lifted modern people from the depression that threatened them, from the anguish of having to live henceforth in a universe deprived of even the slightest intensity of being. But no, matter was now charged! Difference would be inscribed into nature, coursing through life and thought. This wasn't Aristotle's ancient potential. It was a potential for charge, a differential that sparked a current, something that departed, that became, that ripped through flat, extended Being, that made matter quiver. It was something that explained sensation and reinstated its worth. But electricity as recognised by European science was not irrational. Although it apparently escaped inert matter and visible movement, electricity was susceptible to observation and indirect measurement. It was not an abstract metaphysical idea or an impossible-to-prove principle. Electricity reintroduced an intensity into the modern rationalist conception of the world, which measured the world by cutting it into pieces. Electricity provided something new for measurement, a flow of energy.

We can confirm that until the eighteenth century an idea of intensity existed, but it lacked an image. The more or less white wall, the more or less charitable spirit, and the more or less bright day fell under the category of scholastic quarrels that, despite being important in theory, did not touch human sentiment. And then a dazzling image intervened in the history of our representations. As we have seen, the idea of this image proved to be deceptive. Rationalised by science, having lost its mystery and finding itself reduced to the precise properties of matter, electricity did not keep its theoretical promises. At the end of the day, electricity was nothing more than the displacement of tiny elementary parts of charged matter towards the interior of a conductive material due to the effect of a difference in potential.

So it seems that a strange and secret alliance developed in the modern spirit between an image in need of an idea and an idea lacking an image. Discredited by classical rationalism, the idea of pure intensity became abstract, as though it had risen above the relics of Aristotelianism and Scholasticism, beyond qualitative change and the latitude of forms. In the world reconstructed by new physics, we struggled to rationally represent what an intensity was. The intensity of electric current was a spectacular image that thrilled the European public when electricity was discovered. However, as we studied, analysed, and quantified the phenomenon, electric current, which had seemed to be a magical and rational new image of change, an image of an energising discharge that was at once an image of desire, the very image of life itself, appeared to correspond to an equally deceptive idea.

Without any consultation, the image of electricity passed into the ancient idea of intensity, and the dated idea of intensity took shape within the modern electric image. This resulted in a new concept, the first traces of which can be found in German Idealism through Kant, Schelling, and Hegel, and which later became the main character on the philosophical scene in the modern metaphysics of Nietzsche, Bergson, Whitehead, and Deleuze.

From then on, 'intensity' simultaneously meant the variation of a quality, the measure for comparing a thing with itself, the measure of change or becoming, and a pure difference that allowed us to explain the sensitivity and desire of the living. Intensity was what justified the liveability of life and the value of all that escaped quantity and extension – it was an electric brilliance.

If we undertake a quick genealogy of how intensity became a principle of modern life, we find that the ideal that orients our existence is the child of an extremely abstract idea and an absolutely concrete image. The idea and the image merged into one another in order to breathe new life into an old theoretical question, clothing it in the flashing brilliance of electric intensity, and animating the reality of electricity with an occult metaphysical quality.

An unheard-of new concept was born from this alliance.

Notes

1. In 'Whence Intensity? Deleuze and the Revival of a Concept', Mary Beth Mader traces the history of intensity from Aristotle through Deleuze. Her piece makes an excellent companion to this and the following chapter. Mader's and Garcia's discussions supplement one another in fruitful ways, but her article is also an excellent bibliographic resource for most of Garcia's philosophical references. The discussion of intensive versus extensive magnitude from Kant to Deleuze in A. W. Moore's *The Evolution of Modern Metaphysics: Making Sense of Things* is a very useful resource as well.

2. This 'thanks to . . .', a locution that recurs throughout this chapter, is a translation of the French *grâce à*. In a manner wholly befitting Garcia's literary style, this turn of phrase should be read in all of its ambiguity. The entity that receives thanks in each instance (potential, force, and so on) has played an essential role in the development of our understanding of the world. Nevertheless, that position of centrality also makes those entities' inability to provide a totalising explanation of the world all the more glaring. In this sense, Garcia's 'thanks to . . .' also smacks of its ironic parallel: 'Thanks a lot . . . for nothing.'

3. Aristotle, *Categories*, section 3b32.

4. This is the third Rule of Reasoning in Newton's *Principia*.

5. We need to thank François Raffoul and Charles Pence for help with translating Newtonian terminology in these passages.

6. Quoted in Schmiechen, *Newton's Principia Revisited*, p. 128.

7. Quoted in Hankins, *Jean d'Alembert: Science and the Enlightenment*, p. 3.

8. This made it into Chapter 6 ('Classical Mechanics') of Poincaré's *Science and Hypothesis*, with slightly different wording: 'This law of Newton in its turn ceases to be regarded as an experimental law, it is now only a definition. But as a definition it is insufficient, for we do not know what mass is. It enables us, no doubt, to calculate the ratio of two forces applied at different times to the same body, but it tells us nothing about the ratio of two forces applied to two different bodies.'

9. The quoted passage seems to be a paraphrase of language taken from the first in a series of German-language physics textbooks by Klaus Dransfeld et al. See Dransfeld, Kienle, and Kalvius, *Physik I: Mechanik und Wärme*, p. 72.

10. This is a remarkable paragraph precisely because what Garcia claims about force here with respect to classical physics also holds for his treatment of intensity with respect to the metaphysics of *Form and Object*. Here Garcia is affirming that this is a problem for all explanations of a certain type, which is (as argued in the Translators' Introduction) surely part of the reason behind his reversal of the order of *Form and Object* in this trilogy and his decision to end the book in a final aporia. Note also that what Garcia is gesturing at above is an instance of the OOO paradox elucidated in Cogburn's *Garcian Meditations*.

11. This is a reference to Theodor Adorno's defence in his *Aesthetic Theory* of Wilhelm von Humboldt's reproaching a landscape for not being beautiful enough due to an insufficiency of trees. Adorno argues that Humboldt's reaction is paradigmatic insofar as judgements of beauty involve an apprehension of the extent to which things ought to be different from what they really are. He holds that to judge something beautiful is to praise it for being what it really is, and that to judge the opposite is to reproach it for failing to be what it is. Garcia's own account of beauty in Chapter XII of *Form and Object* entails Adorno's position. See also Cogburn's discussion connecting Garcia's accounts of beauty, truth, and goodness in Chapter 9 of *Garcian Meditations*. As noted in the Translators' Introduction, intensity is central to Garcia's notions of beauty, truth, and goodness.

3

A Concept

'We Must Interpret Everything in Terms of Intensity'

The intensity exception

What, exactly, is the concept of intensity in European, and especially German, philosophies of the nineteenth century? It is the representation of an intensity with an irreducible character that is no longer a flaw to be rectified, but rather a quality to be defended. That is, intensity became a completely distinct metaphysical concept, an alliance between qualitative change, the idea of *more or less*, and the attractive image of electric current. Thought was then tasked with distinguishing qualitative changes from measurable quantities. The astonishing example of electricity inverted our whole way of thinking. While intensity had once appeared to be a gap in our understanding, the irreducibility of intense things to quantities now seemed like an opportunity.

From the nineteenth century on, the concept of 'intensive magnitude' tends to designate the measure of something that cannot be ascertained through the use of numbers, the decomposition of space into parts, or the increase or decrease of a quantity. This sort of decomposition and this system of quantities held sway during the reign of the concept of extension, but they were then countered by the concept of intensity. Intensity brought together everything that had escaped 'extensive magnitude'.

Regardless of the domain in which a thing is considered, 'intense' becomes a way of designating whatever presents itself as a whole without being the sum of several distinguishable parts. The intense is immediate and not successive. It is what has a size but cannot be rendered numerically, and it can change without corresponding to a

series of distinct states. That which has value but cannot immediately
be compared to another thing is intense. It is continuous and non-
discrete. It is what springs forth from the intimate, interior experience
of perception, and not from the observable, exterior character of a
phenomenon. Intensity becomes a citadel, a stronghold of resistance
against extension, space, number, quantity, equivalency, exchange,
rationalism, and universalisation. Science is devoted to knowledge
and looks to model everything that appears more than once and
everything that repeats itself. Whereas science is concerned with
providing models for experience in general and its laws, intensity is
instead the measure of the singular and its internal variations.

In this way, intensity was made into the exception *par excellence*.
Intense things were taken to be exceptions to the rationalistic model
of the world. They would heretofore be left to their fate as singular, intimate perceptions. In most of nineteenth-century metaphysics, extension and intensity are opposed to each other and logically
complete one another. Reason gives each of them their due. The
objectivity of the external world, the objectivity of nature as it is perceived, and the objectivity of matter and objects belong to extension;
to intensity, the subjectivity of internal experience and the subjective
perception of nature, spirit, and qualities are granted.

For example, in Kant's 'Analytic of Principles', 'intensive magnitude' signifies what perception can expect from phenomena. By
'extensive magnitude' we mean to say that a phenomenon can be
divided into pieces, that the whole of the phenomenon may be
obtained by putting those pieces together,[1] and that those pieces are
countable and calculable. While intuition can grasp the extensive
magnitude of phenomena in this way, perception instead expects
that both the sensation and the real contained by phenomenon's
object will have an 'intensive magnitude'. Perception understands
the object of a phenomenon in terms of degree.

Leaving aside an exhaustive account of the implications of
this reasoning for the Kantian system, let us at least hold on to
this: the process of making the world inherited from Newton
accessible to experimentation, knowable, and ultimately liveable
requires that each part perceived of this flattened world should be
invested from within with a degree, an intensity. A purely formal
understanding of phenomena is possible when this intensity is

reduced to zero. The reality of the object withdraws until it is reduced to nothing, and only the form of the object remains knowable. However, in perception, the reality of this object is affected by a coefficient.[2] This coefficient is not an extensive magnitude, meaning that it cannot be arrived at piece by piece. Reality affects us *all of a sudden.* The totality of the feeling of reality hits us all at once, and only then is it possible to try to analyse it and measure its variation. But this intensive magnitude is really a kind of barometer internal to subjective experience. It immediately indicates the *degree of appearance* of what is.

The Kantian operation became absolutely crucial. From then on, intensity would designate the degree of internal replenishment of the extensive, exterior world offered up to scientific knowledge. This degree of engagement is nothing other than reality, and is itself dependent upon time. Indeed, Kant's intensive magnitude is bound up with internal, temporal meaning, just as his extensive magnitude is tied to external, spatial meaning.

Say I am looking at the sky. With the passage of time, a feeling of detachment causes the blue and white sky that I contemplate to seem less and less real, and to do so without changing. Only the consciousness with which I regard the object has increased. In these instances of suspense, I feel the feeling of my own gaze rise within me. I have the impression of being something like a movie screen for myself, and representation wins out over what is represented. Sometimes it is enough to blink my eyes, and the sky reappears like a distant truth. I am seized once again by the light that traverses feeling and reaches all the way to the nebulous limits of the earthly atmosphere there high above. The presence and the existence of this feeling fill me with a mild sense of vertigo. I feel the sky as it moves away from my retina. It swells until I find myself surrounded.

The reflexive sensation of representation and the ecstatic feeling of perception beyond the self are joined together in a power dynamic. That power dynamic can be imagined like a continuous line, and variations of the *degree of intensity of the real* can be charted along its length. For Kant, this intensity can decrease to zero, at which point it indicates the victory of pure consciousness over its object. Nevertheless, a definitive maximal intensity capable of marking the triumph of the perceived over perception does not exist. There is the empty form of our possible perception of the world, and there is the real that fills in that form. This real can give the impression of existing more or less, or of being more or less strong, inasmuch as it corresponds to the feeling of intensity that accompanies our perceptions. All of this heralds the existence of an incessant power dynamic between pure consciousness and maximum reality. What we call the real becomes an intensive replenishment of the subject's consciousness. Sometimes it grows weaker, sometimes stronger. And whether it is in a state of sleeplessness, half-sleep, reverie, or extreme lucidity, our intimate experience never stops trying to size up the real.

While Kant's aim is to think the possibility of an intensity equal to zero and allow us to determine the conditions of a pure consciousness emptied of all intensity of reality,[3] we must consider the following contrary hypothesis: at the end of the day, *modern life will have been the search for a maximal intensity of reality*, which is to say a strong experience of an internal welling up and over of the perceived world. In order for us to feel alive, this experience has to swell up and brim over its own boundaries. The perceived has to win out over reflexive perception. The perceived must drown perception beneath the maximal certitude of what I see, touch, and love. That is, the certitude of all of this increases to the extent that there is also a decrease in my awareness of my own gaze, of my nerves, of my heart, of my imprisonment in myself, of my reflection as a conscious subject condemned to perceive a universe filled with deception, a universe in which any point is equal to whichever other point.

I know that nothing is more or less. I know that everything exists equally, but I *feel* differently: I *feel* that all that I perceive can vary in intensity.[4]

A savage exception

As for Kant and Hegel, as soon as the latter defines 'extensive quantum' and 'intensive quantum' in the *Science of Logic*, intensity is taken to be an exception within the realm of extension. But intensity is also placed on a level playing field with extension itself, acting as its partner, guarantor, and counterpart. In European thought of the time, intensity and extension formed a balanced couple. This intensity corresponded to an idea that had already been tamed, having been carefully distinguished from extension and harmoniously wedded to the same. One might even say that this idea of intensity had been 'domesticated' by the concept.

What is most proper to intensity is its irreducibility, meaning that intensity loses its own character when it is reduced to being a complement to extension. The metaphysicians thought that a process would inevitably end by beginning anew. That notion prompted them to attempt to use thought as a means of saving intensity from its recuperation and domestication. True intensity had to be something radically different from that other thing, the one that was supposed to be intensity, but which all too quickly ended up associated with extension.

How to illustrate this? A child softly pinches my skin, which tickles me. Then the pinching presses harder, she grabs more of my skin, and the rather agreeable sensation escalates until it becomes annoying, then grows tiresome, and finishes up being painful. As the intensity of the sensation increases, it leads to an alteration and qualitative transformation of the sensation as it changes from tickling to pain. When Bergson became interested in this specific characteristic of states of consciousness and perception, he was careful to show that the idea of a measurable magnitude of intensity comes from the way in which the mind represents a sensation's cause.[5] Presuming that the cause (the pinch) is extensive, that it occupies space and is measurable (I can determine the variation of the force put into the pinch by the child), the idea of quantity is transposed from the cause of the sensation to the sensation itself. Having once been nothing more than a certain colouring of the quality of my sensation, the intensity of the pinch becomes a magnitude, a measurable size. The projection of my psychic states on to space gives them a form that can be cut into pieces and quantified.

Leaning on this analysis, Bergson forwards a rational critique of the usage of the very term intensity in psychology, and this allows him to distinguish between two types of multiplicity. There is a quantitative, discrete, and numerical multiplicity, and there is a qualitative and continuous multiplicity. Everything that 'takes up space' belongs to the first multiplicity, but the second multiplicity resists and escapes spatialisation. Space as a principle of differentiation is not the same as qualitative differentiation. In space, everything is distinguished by number, but there are no distinct qualities. As we have said, this is the result of the relegation of Cartesian and Newtonian space to a bygone era. This means that the principle of qualitative differentiation is not spatial. For Bergson, qualitative differentiation is instead understood in terms of what he called 'duration', an indistinct and even indivisible multitude of heterogeneous states of the world. And there you have it, authentic intensity, a pure exception.

In other words, Bergson's strategic manoeuvre consists of showing that what we call 'intensity' is just a domesticated form of true intensity. In order to think the concept of intensity, it is necessary to throw yourself into the modern struggle against the taming of the intensive and its reduction to the non-intensive. We must wield thought in the fight to preserve intensity's exceptional character.

Our quick genealogy shows that the very nature of the concept of intensity came from an alliance between the idea of qualitative change and the flashing image of electricity. This lent to the concept something wild and impossible to domesticate. Something is intense if it escapes categorisation and resists reduction. Thought failed in its first attempts at describing the function of this concept as a simple complement to extension. It is not enough to make a distinction in terms of extension between intensity and the principle by which things are extensively distinguished. If such were to be the case, extension would simultaneously end up determining the distinction and being itself determined by that very same distinction.[6]

Thinking of intensity as an exception to extension and localising intensity in subjectivity alone is the same as assigning a place to what has no place. Rather than negating the *idea* within the concept of intensity, thinking of intensity in this way instead negates the *image* that intensity inherited from its electric ancestors. What is lost is the image of a violent discharge, the image of something indomitable that cannot be grasped or classified by thought.

When modern metaphysicians carefully introduced the concept of intensity into their grand systems of classification and distinction, they were unaware that they were letting a fox into the henhouse. In this way, the very principle capable of destroying all classification and all distinction was introduced into their vast charts and schemas.

The exception becomes the rule

How and why did the concept of intensity stop representing a simple metaphysical exception? Intensity allowed us to conceive of a world composed of entities that were individuated, but not withdrawn into themselves. The ancient notion of substance certainly made it possible to single out and describe things such as the man, the tree, and the table. However, substance also produced the notion of things in themselves. These sorts of things served as the supports or substrata for change, but they themselves were not subject to change. Above all, potential found itself locked away inside substances. Classical force, on the other hand, was a universal, liberated potential with measurable effects. This classical notion of force was at once unique and impersonal, and it acted upon a lacklustre, homogeneous kind of matter, one devoid of intensity.

Intensities are simultaneously individuated and not in themselves. They combine the advantages of potential and those of force, making intensity a qualified form of force. This means that it is no longer necessary to think that any quality underlies the variation of intensity because *intensity's variation is itself a quality*.

Intensity freed itself from the constraints of prior definitions and went from being an exception to being a rule. This is the revelation: everything is intense, and intensity is everything! Like a reflection on the surface of water, a tree that is identical to itself is nothing but an effect of the profound reality of that which is, continuous variations of being, lines of becoming that momentarily appear like stable objects in space. But if I think that everything is made of intensities, then there is no longer any tree. All that remains are the processes by which the tree 'trees itself'. And one fine day, it will 'untree itself'. The tree will fall, and its components will decompose. The tree already loses some of its parts every autumn; a leaf falls, and a little of its bark is eroded by the wind. What I call the tree is nothing but a knot of being, a tangling of lines of becoming. The tree is a knotting of lines of intensity from the earth, an earth that gives and takes moisture. The knotted lines stem from the growing forest, from the rising sap, from the exchanges of energy that occur between the living organism and its environment, and so on.

By a value reversal typical of the modern mind, intensity, which was once an exception to extension, instead became a name for everything that is. Extension then became an exception to intensity.

This new vision of a world made of intensities made its presence felt in several different philosophical systems. Nietzsche, Whitehead, and Deleuze each envisioned a universe that was no longer extended and composed of discrete parts that could be assembled into a whole.[7] They instead proposed a purely intensive universe with apparently stable parts that are nothing but illusions generated by our limited perception.

The world of Nietzschean potential is thus the gripping representation of a single intensity. Its image is that of an immense ocean that persists without external aid. According to this image, there is nothing outside that ocean of intensity. To see this, imagine a single, immense, variable intensity of all that is. In order to take itself as an object, this being splits, returns to itself, and appears to divide itself into subject and object. But there is really only ever a vast oceanic intensity. It fluctuates locally, not globally. Everything is intensity in Nietzsche's fragments from *The Will to Power*, and, for this very reason, intensity is absolute. Since intensity is absolute, its sum does not vary. And from all of this it follows that everything is intense (because everything fluctuates) except intensity, which is itself absolute (and does not fluctuate).[8] It is an ocean of forces unleashed with neither beginning nor end. Intensity is a mass that grows neither larger nor smaller, it is 'a household without expenses or losses, but likewise without increase or income'.[9] Intensity is at once singular and plural when it competes against itself. It becomes individuated and divides itself into multiple intensities. Intensity varies all the while, increasing in some places and decreasing by the same amount in others.

So, according to Nietzsche, nothing is non-intense except the absolute totality of intensity itself. What *inside the world* seems non-intense, and therefore also resolutely stable and identical, is just the illusory effect of a weak intensity. Intensity really has no opposite because the non-intense is just the weakest degree of the intensity of being. Here 'intensity' refers to the absolutisation of variation, which once seemed to be the opposite of the absolute. Only variation itself does not vary. The apparent permanence of an object, concept, or idea is just a ruse of universal intensity. That intensity may decrease in one location, and make room for experimenting with one of its own infinite possibilities. This is why twentieth-century Nietzscheans such as Foucault exchanged the notion of a constitutive subject for that of a 'process of subjectification'. That whole process is fundamentally born out of historical variations with different moments that can be traced through the genealogical method. Deep down, no being is identical to itself. Intensities are all there is. The prioritisation of fundamental principles becomes inverted; intensities are natural and primary, and so-called 'identities' are constructed and secondary.

And yet this conception served as an implicit ontology (which is to say, a theory on the very being of things) for many of those in modernity who no longer wanted anything to do with ontology. They argued that nothing exists in itself outside of our perception. Nothing is identical – everything differs, everything is intense! Nothing exists beyond the intense. The apparent stability of our representations of simple, invariable, permanent, and eternal entities is a product of our limited historical perception. These representations create the illusion of being absolutely non-intense, when the truth is that they are merely *weakly* intense.

Inasmuch as there is just one immense intensity, that intensity cannot be compared with anything else. Such an intensity can neither increase nor decrease. This means that being in its totality can never exist more or less. Intensity becomes multiple inside a world. An intensity can increase inside a world as long as another intensity decreases along with it. And what is the world, we might ask? It is nothing other than a zero-sum game of intensities.

So that's Nietzsche in a nutshell. Nevertheless, this first vision of a universal and eternal intensity was replaced by another. Instead of a zero-sum game, this second vision posited a process which was intense, but still capable of creation. This second vision is perhaps best expressed by Whitehead. In his *Process and Reality*, the multiple intensities of being participate in the general process by which being itself constantly appears in novel variations. Everything is intense. Everything changes. Everything is the provisional 'concrescence' of multiple intensities. Multiplicities harmonise and unite, and the resulting unity is added to the multiplicity. Molecules are like dynamic societies of atoms. But those societies of atoms are themselves also dynamic societies of protons and electrons, which societies are likewise societies of more elementary particles or force vectors. Each element is in fact a result, but it is not a simple arithmetical sum. What we have instead is an active totality that transforms its own parts in the same way that a molecule in formation acts on the state of the atoms that compose it. The very relationship between two entities is added to the list as yet another entity.[10] A new tension becomes possible between the two former terms and the newly arrived third term. Active concepts are always preferred in Whitehead's ontology. He elevates *concrescence*, which is a process, above *concretum*, the result achieved by that process. This simple grammatical phenomenon makes the point clear. We often identify philosophies of intensity by their systematic preference for the usage of present participles such as *constituting* or *creating* over past participles such as *constituted* or *created*. Being is from the beginning a process, not the end of a process. This vision of creative intensity guided all of the modern minds that refused the notion that the being of nature was 'always already' constituted. They instead insisted that something made out of parts was the *work* of becoming, and never its *origin*. From this it seems that intensity is not a tension between two identities. If that were the case, it would be as though we started with fixed entities, only to mechanically attach them in a relationship at a later point. But the truth is that all of the apparent identities in the world are the product of intensities, as it were; a *variant* is the product of a *variable*, and not the other way around.

Deleuze provides us with a third and final vision of intensity. His 'intensity' allows us to give a name to this kind of variation, 'pure difference', a difference of difference. We will recall that electrical intensity had to do with a difference of potential between two poles. But Deleuze shows in *Difference and Repetition* that the intensity that scientists talk about is not exactly the same as the intensity of the metaphysicians. Electrical intensity is nothing more than a physical index used to represent true intensity. Because if electrical intensity requires a difference in charge, we must also conclude that each charge is itself the result of a difference. But metaphysical intensity goes even further. By 'intensity', we do not mean the difference between two identifiable entities. Intensity is instead the difference between two terms that themselves are nothing more than an effect of the difference between two terms, which terms are themselves also nothing more than ... and so on and so forth.

In each of these three visions, we see that intensity is crowned and elevated to its status as foremost among the qualities of being through a clever reversal. It was once thought that intensity was an effect caused by our perception of an extended, quantifiable, and measurable world. But now it seems that the reality of things is fundamentally intensive, and that the extensive appearance of things is nothing more than an effect of that reality. Everything is intense, but our perception makes use of cognition, language, and grammar to produce different stabilising effects. Those stabilising effects cause the intense universe to *appear* to us as a totality of distinct objects in space that can be identified again and again over time.

In order to banish this illusion, it is necessary to follow Deleuze's lead and 'interpret everything as intensities'. In fact, not just these metaphysical visions, but all human knowledge now runs headlong into an implicit injunction. In antiquity, humanity was brought up to live in a universe of substances, and in the classical age, humanity inhabited a world governed by force. But in the modern age, little by little, humanity became accustomed to living in a world of intensities, and all our knowledge was again reorganised in response to this demand.

Interpreting everything in terms of intensity

Metaphysical representations such as these of purely intense worlds can seem abstract. Nevertheless, the crisis of our knowledge's classificatory categories is a direct and verifiable effect of this metaphysical intensification.

We now inhabit a world that is no longer made of substances and qualities.[11] We have instead come to think that, when we get to the bottom of things, differences, variations, and intensities are all that exist. And for that very reason, modernity in the life sciences progressively led to a rejection of the classification of organisms piece by piece. This happened because it no longer seemed reasonable to think of organisms as belonging to fixed species, as if science could divide up all of space into a vast display case where every species could be viewed at once, each in its separate compartment. Such a conception of classification fitted with the classical age, but there was no room for it in the modern project. Most of the systems of knowledge produced by the modern avant-garde implicitly held that the most real things in the world were made up of variations, rather than consisting of simple, fixed, permanent substances. They endeavoured to see and interpret organic and inorganic reality in terms of intensities and variations rather than stable identities. For example, in general relativity, physical objects no longer determine the lines of the universe. On the contrary, the lines of the universe are what define physical objects. In the same way, our attempts to understand living things through the neo-Darwinian theory of evolution led us to abandon the classification and organisation of organisms into fixed species. The study of processes of 'speciation' was preferred instead. There are no longer any specific essences. There is nothing but the continuously varying liminal effects of the different branches of the general evolution of life. So, how are we to divide a simple and fixed notion of humanity into all of the variable intensities of life? Classification can no longer justify this magical operation for this reason: classification can draw genealogical lines through the totality of living things, but it is incapable of staking out the frontiers of that totality. We think of a line as an unbroken geometrical reality, and modernity likewise prompts us to think about progressive changes rather than the fixed underpinnings of those changes. There is no longer an inviolable species demarcation between humanity and other animals. Humanity itself *is* now just a line marking variation.[12]

Since that time, our knowledge has made us pay more attention to these intensities than to the limits between different extensions.

The modern question is no longer that of where humanity begins and ends. The question has now become the following: what is a person made of and how can that person become something else?

Just as processes of speciation took the place of species, gender and sex also made room for processes of sexuation and 'genderification'.[13] It is hardly possible any longer to talk about men and women as absolutely separate parts of a whole called humanity. After all, deep within ourselves, and underneath the masks of gender performativity, there is nothing to be found but variable intensities. Now all that can be said is that 'this feminises itself more or less' or 'this masculinises itself more or less'. Genders are no longer nouns; they are verbs because they correspond to acts. They are intensive realities. Our knowledge and modern practices are founded on this principle; identities are always effects; what really exists are intensities. Intensity went from being an exception to being the cardinal rule of our systems of knowledge. We have come to think that what really exists outside our categorisations and cultural constructions are not identities but rather differences, incessant variations, fluctuations, and developments.

But this principle of our knowledge has a history. Our taste for genealogies also has its own genealogy. Our distrust regarding all that seems fixed, absolute, and eternal is itself neither fixed, absolute, nor eternal. All of this is bound up with our type, or one might even say our *style*, of humanity. Our version of humanity has adopted the concept of intensity as the implicit principle behind all of our knowledge.

Our knowledge became particularly attentive to intensities – of species and genre – in order to begin deconstructing classic identities. The fact that everything that had been identified in this way then had to be dissolved into more fundamental intensities made this an endless process. As soon as knowledge had identified an intensity, it became fixed and had to be critiqued in order to show that it was an ideological effect, a social and historical construct. This had to happen so that the real intensities that produced those effects and constructs might show themselves. And this drive to rethink all identities as intensities served as the enthusiastic motor of modern knowledge – until the wheels fell off.

Intensities have to be supported

An unheard of difficulty came to light as the concept of intensity was generalised throughout the arts and sciences of the twentieth century. Paradoxically, it seems that the absolute victory of intensity is also a sign that its defeat is quickly drawing nigh. To make an entity absolute is also to annihilate it. The recognition of the intense character of something manifests this undesirable effect in all domains. Once identified, intensities soon cease to be recognisably intense.[14]

Maybe, at the heart of the very concept of intensity, this is the price we must pay. Conceived as a savage exception to the identical and the quantifiable, intensity only functions as intensification. Identified as intensity, it is no longer itself. And, serving as identity, it ceases to be intense. It is easy to see how the following paradox then takes shape. As a conceptualisation of what escapes identity, intensity cannot be identified without immediately losing the identity it just received. We might simply say that intensity *doesn't sustain itself*. By accessing being, intensity also loses it. Why? Because intensity is the very concept of that which resists conceptualisation. Because it is the concept of what becomes, what differs, and what is inassimilable. Intensity is a concept that resists being something by definition. It seems that making intensity absolute through thought, which is the same as declaring that everything is intense, fatally trends towards the de-intensification of the concept. The more everything is intense, the less this intensity can itself be intense. Intensity is then its own opposite; it becomes a rule, a norm, a universal principle for measuring and dividing the entities of the world. The ancient concept of substance described a being that subsisted in itself and was capable of supporting its own being. By contrast, the concept of intensity designates an evanescent sort of being, one that *is no longer* as soon as it *begins* to be. Such a being never is what it is. It cannot support itself. It disappears as soon as it appears, and that is the price to be paid.

The force of the modern concept of intensity was undoubtedly tied to the fabulous alliance of an idea with the image of electricity. It was this alliance that introduced a sort of savagery and a proud, wild character into the idea, as well as a taste for shock and gripping excitement. This character was drawn from the image of electricity and made it possible to think of the idea of a pure qualitative change as a quality rather than a flaw. When it came time to make room for this new paradoxical concept of intensity, its electric image made it impossible to pin down its idea.

Intensity turned out to be stronger than all of the functions attributed to it. The potential of the electric image generated this strange effect, pure variation, qualitative change, and continuous kinds of things that could no longer be numerically distinguished from quantity, number, and the differentiated. 'Intensity' became the modern name for something irreducible, something eluding the project of providing an extensive rationalistic model of the world. It was up to the modern mind to single out whatever could not be reduced to quantity, and intensity fitted the bill. Intensity was not equivalent in potential to other things, nor could it be exchanged for an identical quantity of those same things. And so, at the end of the day, everything that didn't enter into the count was intense. 'Intensity' thus came to be synonymous with the blind spot of the rationalist undertaking, namely, a principal reliance upon the comparison of a thing with itself. In antiquity, substance had served to support the concept of identity. But now intensity could replace identity, and everything became intense. Therefore, everything became powerful, worthy, and different, but not distinct. Everything had a value, but nothing could be counted, exchanged, or divided into different denominations.[15]

We call something 'intense', and at that very moment it is already less intense than it once was.

Intensity had been made absolute by many of the grand, modern metaphysical systems of intensity (Nietzsche, Whitehead, and Deleuze). Moreover, intensity became an indispensable part of the concrete operations by which human knowledge was able to start categorising processes instead of stable entities. But intensity exposed its conceptual flaw at the very moment of its absolute triumph. Everything came to be represented in terms of intensity, but intensity itself lost all intensity as soon as it was identified. Of course, this de-intensification took time, but it was an inevitable consequence of this very conceptualisation of the intense. Conceiving of intensity in this way leads us to confront the paradox of identity itself.

It seems as if it is the *perception*, not the thought, of intensity that continues to threaten every intensity. An intensity is perceived, and some part of it is immediately lost in the ensuing process of identification and re-identification. All intensities have to accept this trend towards their own neutralisation in order to be perceived. Intensity's constitutive weakness is that it is lost to perception from the very outset. Perception ought to have made it possible to observe and talk about intensity. Instead, it became a secret formula that explains how intensity was transformed from a *metaphysical concept* into a *moral value*. Another history, one not in the domain of abstract knowledge, runs parallel to that of the concept of intensity. This other history tries to lend support to the concept of intensity by accounting for the ideal of intensity in terms of both perception and life.

Our perception kills all intensities, but it also allows them to survive. An intensity becomes incapable of sustaining itself when it is perceived. The intervention of a subject, someone who concretely perceives an intensity, is necessary if that intensity is to be prolonged. No intense world can be sustained without the support of a living being.[16]

We have to fight to maintain intensities. It is not enough to simply perceive the world; we also have to find a way to endlessly manoeuvre within and through intensities, replacing what has been identified with the unidentified. The modern subject could not assess an intense world without causing the haemorrhaging and complete loss of its intensity. The inactivity of a passive, observing, and purely neutral subject quickly empties the world of all intensity. The world meets its end in the exhaustion of complete identification. From the moment that there was a subject in the world, that same subject found itself swept up by an ideal of intensity in its attempts to maintain the constitutive intensity of the world.

The concept of intensity was so seductive to the modern mind that it made subjectivity necessary again. As in Baudelaire's poem, subjectivity was both the dagger and the victim.[17] Subjectivity was once an instrument that destroyed all intensity through the neutralising effects of knowledge, but also the first to suffer as the ravages of that destruction made the world unliveable. But the same victim that suffers for its guilt is also a saviour. Handed over to the perception of the living, even the most intense world ends up becoming completely flat. Only subjectivity could save such a world. Subjectivity took up the search for the intensity of all things as its ideal. It sought out dead intensities, replaced them with living ones, and set about constantly regenerating what was in danger of becoming fossilised through familiarity, habit, and identification. Subjectivity demanded something new, something unheard of, something electric. It went in search of something that made it impossible to freeze becoming into being, to calculate intensities as measurable extensions, and to gauge qualities in terms of quantity.

The intensity of this new world had to be sustained. This called for the formation of a new subject, an intense humanity.

Notes

1. In *The Evolution of Modern Metaphysics*, A. W. Moore shows that, starting at least with Kant and continuing through Deleuze, one of the key differences between extensive and intensive magnitudes is that the former, but not the latter, satisfy what in mathematics is known as the distributive property with respect to addition. That is, for any extensive magnitude m, where x and y are distinct, non-overlapping entities measured by m, we have that $m(x + y) = mx + my$. For example, the spatial extent of two distinct, non-overlapping entities is the sum of the spatial extent of each individual entity. This is *not* the case with magnitudes such as the temperature of objects or the extent to which objects are good instances of various colours. In the context of Garcia's discussion the issue of distributivity is important, because he seems to deny in some places and affirm in others that intensive magnitudes are quantitatively measurable. However, in spite of these appearances, the measurement of intensive magnitudes always involves some failure of distributivity. Garcia in effect shows that the replacement of non-distributive magnitudes by (extensive) distributive ones is a key part of how those magnitudes are subjected to rational prediction and control. In this context, consider the hedonistic utilitarian understanding of the morally optimal act as the one that produces the most pleasure. The 'utilitarian calculus' is possible here precisely because the amount of pleasure derived is taken to be extensive in the sense of satisfying the distributive

property. Now contrast this with the more traditional view that we should realise the true, the good, and the beautiful. Closeness to God (the Thomistic unity of truth, goodness, and beauty) is not distributive. There are simply too many different possible ways to be a scholar, saint, or artist, too many odd combinations of these realised in the same person, and (given our finitude) progress in one area often precludes progress in others. Moreover, the replacement of non-distributive with distributive magnitudes vastly facilitates the marketisation of the phenomena in question. For the utilitarian, the extent to which one act is more valuable than another is a kind of measurable fact. *Form and Object*'s Chapter XI ('Economy of Objects') is an extended meditation on how this very process, stemming from the manner in which utilitarianism allows distributive quantification, undermines spheres that might be autonomous from the market.

2. The astute reader will have noticed the homology between Kant and the Garcia of *Form and Object* here. The formal world of Book I lacks intensity. While intensity does not yield the reality of an object for Garcia, it does yield much of philosophical and practical interest, including events, time, life, truth, beauty, and goodness.

3. Again, consider the homology between Kant and the author of Book I of *Form and Object*. Of course, Garcia is not describing a 'consciousness' devoid of intensity, but rather a world radically independent of consciousness. Nevertheless, just as Kant argued that our non-formal knowledge forces us to presuppose consciousness to be formally articulated in the way that he describes, Garcia argues for the analogous claim with respect to the world.

4. One of the trickiest problems in reading Garcia is determining the extent of his concessions to this kind of Kantianism (see the discussions in Cogburn's *Garcian Meditations*). One should be *very* wary of attributing to Garcia a full-throated endorsement of the Kantian rendering of intensity as subjective. First, such claims always arise for Garcia as part of a dialectical march through the history of various concepts, marches that usually end in aporia and contradiction. Note that in the very next section Garcia mocks the idea of 'localising intensity in subjectivity alone' as 'assigning a place to what has no place'. In any case, how one interprets the dialectical march to contradiction will determine how one interprets these passages. Second, as noted (and explained in *Garcian Meditations*), Garcia's own accounts of time, life, animality, and personhood all utilise the notion of intensity in non-trivial ways. To the extent that Garcia

endorses these accounts (again, they are presented dialectically), he must reject the idea that intensity is a product of human subjectivity. For to simultaneously say with Garcia that humanity is a product of intensity and with Kant that intensity is a product of humanity is to enter the kind of circularity that Garcia refers to as 'compactness' in *Form and Object*. See note 6.

5. For a more complete discussion, with citations, see Moore's *The Evolution of Modern Metaphysics*.

6. According to the metaphysics of *Form and Object*, an entity is that which differentiates the things comprehending that entity and the things which that entity comprehends. This means that comprehension serves as the root notion underlying both mereological composition and property instantiation. 'Compactness' is Garcia's general term of abuse for any putative entity which, to be the kind of thing it would need to be, would have to be subject to a reflexive (a comprehends a) or symmetric (a comprehends b and b comprehends a) comprehension relation. Note that all vicious circles, such as the one alleged above, are instances of compactness. But, as shown in *Garcian Meditations*, compactness is prohibited by Garcia's metaphysics. An entity that is compact would not be differentiated from that which it comprehends and that which comprehends it, because it itself would be in the set of things it was differentiated from.

7. Graham Harman notes that what we refer to as 'process philosophy' comes in two widely divergent forms, reflected in the contrast between Nietzsche and Whitehead that Garcia goes on to make. Schopenhauer, Nietzsche, the British Hegelians, Simondon, and (perhaps) Deleuze all in different ways present a picture of a somewhat amorphous reality more fundamental than the world of individuated objects, which emerge out of that world. These philosophers all follow Spinoza in taking there to be in some sense only one truly individuated thing. Whitehead and Latour, on the other hand, follow Leibniz and radically *increase* the multiplicity of the world. Their take on the process–philosophical conceit that relations are more fundamental than objects ends up in effect treating all of the relations between objects as if they were the real objects. While Harman's object-oriented ontology also entails this, his view is not process philosophy because he holds that everyday, individuated objects (for example, tables and chairs) exist in their own right as self-identical enduring entities. See Harman's 'Whitehead and Schools X, Y, and Z' for a definitive statement on the two types of process philosophy, and his 'Tristan Garcia and the Thing-in-Itself'

for, in effect, an argument that Garcia only avoids the first form of process philosophy by embracing the second. For a defence of Garcia on this point, see Cogburn's *Garcian Meditations*.

8. For a regimentation of an argument from the premise that relations individuate to the conclusion that there is one entity, see the Putnam-Parmenides argument in Chapter 5 of Cogburn's *Garcian Meditations*.

9. Nietzsche, *The Will to Power*, p. 550.

10. The clearest discussion in the English-language philosophical literature of how this works is in Graham Harman's *Prince of Networks: Bruno Latour and Metaphysics*.

11. In analytic philosophy, the closest thing one finds to the Deleuzean view is the 'ontic structural realism' typically defended by some of the people working at the intersection of metaphysics and the philosophy of physics. James Ladyman's *Stanford Encyclopedia* article 'Structural Realism' is helpful in this regard.

12. In *Form and Object*'s Book II, Chapter VI: 'Humans', Garcia traces our evolving conception of ourselves in terms of our relation to divinities and animals on the one hand and the living and the machinic on the other. Just as our concept of ourselves as non-animalian and non-machinic became threatened, we attempted to become divinities by arrogating to ourselves the God-like tasks of teaching animals language and designing intelligent machines.

13. See *Form and Object*'s Book II, Chapter XIV: 'Genders'.

14. One of the running themes of Jonathan Bennett's *Kant's Analytic* is the paradoxical manner in which the transcendental becomes empirical as soon as we start talking about it. Phenomena such as meaningfulness, knowability, thinkability, causation, necessity, obligation, etc. are so all-encompassing that our attempts to provide transcendental accounts of their conditions of possibility always end up being given in terms of the phenomena themselves. If this is correct, it lends itself to a powerful critique of at least a certain kind of marketplace Deleuze, with the intensive slide into the extensive being yet another version of the transcendental slide into the empirical. But one should not read Garcia as arguing that everything is empirical or extensive, which is an old response to this problem. For example, in 'The "Transcendental Method": On the Reception of the *Critique of Pure Reason* in Neo-Kantianism', Konstantin Pollok shows how one of the very first influential neo-Kantians, Friedrich Albert Lange, predated Quine's 'naturalised epistemology' by around a century. In effect turning necessity into a virtue, Lange recast Kant's work as something akin to empirical psychology. But as Garcia (who has more in common with

the school of German Idealism that Lange and the neo-Kantians were rejecting) goes on to instance in what follows, one need not respond to the paradox by changing the subject.

15. In *Form and Object*'s Book II, Chapter XI: 'Economy of Objects', Garcia gives a full account of the paradoxical ways in which we attempt to evade the ever-expanding hegemony of the market.

16. Again (cf. note 4 above) we have Garcia seemingly affirming a Kantian view which, when coupled with the use of intensity in *Form and Object*, would render intensity compact. As before, this is a moment in the dialectic where the Kantian recoil is part of a new understanding of the subject which takes itself to be the locus of intensity. It will also be very clear from Garcia's concluding discussions that he does *not* take the Kantian recoil to have solved the root contradiction at the intersection of thought and life, or the immanent and transcendent (as considered in note 14) for that matter.

17. This is an allusion to the penultimate quatrain in Baudelaire's poem from *Les Fleurs du mal*, 'L'Héautontimorouménos': « Je suis la plaie et le couteau ! / Je suis le soufflet et la joue ! / Je suis les membres et la roue, / Et la victime et le bourreau ! » Baudelaire, *Les Fleurs du mal*, pp. 128–9.

4

A Moral Ideal

The Intense Person

A new type of electric person

A metaphysics of intensity never exists without a morality of intensity. From the beginning, we at least need a heroic subject capable of enduring a world of differences, variations, fluctuations, bursts of energy, and power plays. This subject must relinquish stable identities, eternal ideas, and any hope of respite. It refuses to seek sanctuary from the intense fluctuations of change and rejects the shelter of a reassuring image of the absolute. We must therefore imagine a sort of courageous being stripped of all hypocrisy. Such a being sees the world as it really is and upholds an image where nothing stays as it is and where everything is *more or less*. Such a being sustains the image of a world made up of nothing but intensities. This world conception requires the emergence of a subject that can keep intensities from annulling themselves with the passage of time. Every intensity is evanescent and neutralises itself when it becomes reality, and intense things must be irreducible to being. Subjectivity has to actively help sustain and support all of the intensities that it perceives. That is also why subjectivity has to fight tooth and nail to prevent colour, sounds, ideas, and all of the other intensities that it perceives from waning. Since it is what feels and thinks, subjectivity constantly struggles with its own predilection towards converting intensities into identities and quantities. There has to be an *intense* subjectivity. The image of electricity revealed intensity, and now we need an *electric* subjectivity.

A new type of moral model emerged as the importance of electricity increasingly took hold in modern life. Let us briefly sketch the figure of this moral model, this *electric person*. This is a being that is indifferent to the promises of grace and the search for salvation or truth. The electric person is not waiting for another life to ease her mind about this one; her existence is not guided by the thought of another one that will be better. This being focuses her efforts in a single direction, one where mirror images of the same body and the same life are traversed by a current that grows stronger and stronger. This person does not compare her perceptions to ideas. Instead, she looks to what she perceives for a means of comparing perceptions to themselves. She does this in order to increase the stimulation of perceptions, charging them until they become more vivid and scintillating. The electric person does not fixate on any relationship between beings. She reproaches nothing and no one for not being what they aren't. She only urges them to be what they already are, but in the most energetic, effulgent way possible. For the electric person, nothing in nature is in itself degrading or unworthy of existence. Everything that exists can and must exist, even nature's apparent monstrosities. However, everything must try to *be* with all of the energy it can muster. As an organic being, our person is called to intensify her nature. Everything must be intensi-fied: vital functions, metabolism, the five senses and the ability to enjoy things, empathy, and autonomy. She finds no faults in her own being, or at least thinks that her own are no greater than those of anyone else. The electric person is not interested in absolutes because, for her, there is no end to the process of self-actualisation; she just wants to actualise her being as vigorously as possible. She aims for a maximum degree of perfection and intensification of her faculties, sensations, and conceptions. By 'intense' or 'electric' person, we mean an avant-garde form of humanity that emerged in the eighteenth century and willingly accepted that life exists on a gradient between the body and thought. For the electric person, life happens on a spectrum that straddles her physiology and her mind. This form of humanity has an insatiable craving for social, erotic, political, and scholarly experiences. Those experiences allow the electric person to sustain the intensity of her perceptions in a fight to the death against boredom, petty manipulations, normalcy, identification, and later, in the twentieth century, against a modern sort of bureaucratisation of existence.

Modernity's intense person is wary of tradition. If the modern mind demanded novelty, it was mostly for this reason: the body and mind are a blazing chalice fuelled by intensity. They are ever crying out for new intensities to consume; all the while, old intensities pass from the embers of the unknown to the ashes of the already-identified. The world loses its charge of intensity unless we constantly recharge it.

The libertine, person of nerves

While thinking about 'more and more men of his time' and the humanity of the future, Sade writes,

> We wish to be roused, stirred, they say, 'tis the aim of every man who pursues pleasures, and we would be moved by the most active means. Taking our departure from this point, it is not a question of knowing whether our proceedings please or displease the object that serves us, it is purely a question of exposing our nervous system to the most violent possible shock; now, there is no doubt that we are much more keenly affected by pain than by pleasure: the reverberations that result in us when the sensation of pain is produced in others will essentially be of a more vigorous character, more incisive, will more energetically resound in us, will put the animal spirits more violently into circulation and these, directing themselves toward the nether regions by the retrograde motion essential to them, instantly will ignite the organs of voluptuousness and dispose them to pleasure.[1]

Sade discovered that the cause or object of a nervous shock is always less decisive than its intensity. Ultimately, whether we make the 'object that serves us' feel pleasure or pain, delight or suffering, joy or sadness, the only thing that counts is the intensity of what we feel. Even a violent fit of suffering from another person can electrify and wake up our senses, priming them for pleasure. A grand Sadean notion is that pleasure has less to do with pleasure itself and more to do with the force of pleasure or pain (and we might also note that pain 'affects us much more keenly than pleasure'). Living things see excitement as a fundamental value, and as such we abstract it from both its object and whatever moral or immoral character we or anyone else might attribute to it in any particular instance. We may also feel greater pleasure during a strong sensation of pain than we would feel from a lesser pleasure without an additional sensation of pain. The intensity of feeling is the only absolute measure of life. Living things feel themselves live as a result of the force of the shocks that they undergo. A living being that is numb may suffer less, but it also feels less and lives less. This Sadean rule is driven by the discovery of the electric nature of sensitive bodies. The nerves of the body are suffused with electricity. The intensity of the organism varies in accordance with the excitation of the nerves, and this makes it possible to explain how a being can feel as if it exists more or less. 'Pleasure is but the shock of voluptuous atoms or atoms emanating from voluptuous objects inflaming the electric particles that circulate in the hollows of our nerves. So, for pleasure to be complete, the shock must be as violent as possible', explains the libertine Saint-Fond to Juliette in Sade's novel.[2]

The eighteenth-century libertine engaged with the believer and the philosopher as both adversary and interlocutor. The libertine promotes a materialist conception of the universe, and she is adept at amorous and sexual experimentation. But most importantly, the libertine embodies the first *electric person* of Western modernity. Nervosity, or more precisely, the essentially nervous character of life, is an obvious demonstration of the current that runs through human organisms. Just like other sentient animals that feel suffering and pain, humanity is a bundle of nerves. The libertine strives to model her existence to fit with this nervous excitability. The libertine makes her nerves into what Diderot famously called the 'sensitive fibres' in *Le Rêve de d'Alembert*. They resonate like vibrating strings and transform her body into something like a living harpsichord.[3] From Don Juan to Casanova, from Crébillon's characters to those of Laclos, and from the first materialists to Sade, the character of this intense kind of humanity is that of a nervous being who learns to experiment on others and herself to intensify the physical feeling of her own existence. Recognising no moral norm but the intensification of this feeling, the libertine desires neither a life after death nor a life in death. No, the libertine only wants to live twice as much in this precise sense; the libertine wants to live twice as much as the ordinary person. We already see this theme in Condillac, who writes that 'it seems to him that his being increases and he gains a double existence'.[4]

First as a seventeenth-century materialist philosopher, and then as an experimenter in the salons of the eighteenth century, the libertine served as the avant-garde for a form of humanity that hoped to live *more*. This type of humanity attuned what it knew, desired, and believed to its nerves. It measured the force of the objects of its senses and thoughts by the intensity of the vibrations rattling through its nervous system.

The libertine is a person capable of sustaining the intensity of her own organism. Such a person deduces the value of all truths from the greater or lesser excitation of the nerves of the body. For a living body, the only objective is that of measuring the intensity of that which strikes the nerves and produces pleasure or pain. This morality does not demand that actions be assessed without appeal to absolute, eternal ideas. It is instead necessary to evaluate the intensity of the impressions and ideas that strike us in terms of the currents that their impact generates throughout our nervous system.

The romantic, person of storms

The libertine's nerves soon branched out beyond her body to take root in the whole of nature. In some ways, the romantic is a libertine who, having deserted cities and salons, discovers outside of her body a sort of nervosity belonging to all of nature. The nervosity of nature is often revealed by storms, which is why the romantic is the poet of storms and passions, of *Sturm und Drang*. The intense person of the end of the eighteenth century and the beginning of the nineteenth century upholds an ideal of natural intensity that resonates in the same way throughout the nerves of the body and the vault of the sky. We see this evoked in the stanzas that Lord

Byron composed in the midst of a violent storm: 'Clouds burst, skies flash, oh, dreadful hour!'[5] 'Rise quickly, longed-for storms!' René exclaims.[6] 'The storm comes tomorrow', Hugo seems to respond.[7]

The romantic poet's revelation is often accompanied by a first love. Like the sudden revelation of electricity in nature, the thunder and lightning of that amorous shock to the system recharge the romantic's own internal electricity.

Libertines and romantics end up embodying two models of the moral ideal that Jean Deprun refers to as 'intensivism'.[8] According to him, intensivism simultaneously joins together a conception of time, happiness, and personhood, and at this point we can already see the traces of Rousseau and Sade. This conception stems from the discovery of a self-identity that is no longer substantial. This kind of self-identity instead arises from the joint movement of the nerves and the soul, and gives expression to profound fluctuations of personality. This movement is akin to the roiling currents found in the depths of the ocean. The doctor of Sèze notes the following in his physiological and philosophical research on animal sensitivity and life, 'By this sensation at the root of all others [...] one is thus assured that one exists, not only because one knows it, but because one feels it. This feeling, strong in childhood, is lost, or rather, confused in the soul's tumultuous movements following adulthood.'[9] From Maine de Biran to Cabanis, seventeenth-century thinkers were obsessed with this *feeling of self*. Biran located the absolute feeling of self in the intensity of effort. A person on the verge of drowning acquires a lively and incontestable feeling of existing and being herself. Abstract thought can never account for such a feeling with any certainty.

How can we be sure that we are really ourselves? The libertine and romantic models of intense humanity respond to this crucial question through action. For them, pure thought cannot provide any assurances regarding our identity or our correspondence with ourselves for this reason: identity is no longer substantial; identity is intensive. I have to deal with the fact that my social life makes me less myself. It distances me from the maximal sensation of myself. Only a vigorous interior movement, an effort on the part of a whole being, can resist this torpor and restore the self's most

profound meaning and highest degree of actualisation. Libertinism and Romanticism turn out to have been vast moral, amorous,
and political laboratories. Therein was carried out the project of
maintaining the intense feeling of existence and reinforcing that
feeling against the onslaught of age and integration into a society that constantly threatens to weaken it. In antiquity, happiness
was identified with the absence of troubles, with peace, or with
ataraxia. But in the Enlightenment, this classical notion of happiness is overcome by a powerful and agitated feeling of life. As
Madame de Staël writes, 'A greater intensity of life is always an
enhancement of happiness.'[10] This intensity of life is a new feeling
in the nerves. In the mind of the romantic, this feeling renews the
links between interior and exterior nature and serves to bring the
storm and the self together through an energetic analogy.

   In the unleashed elements, the romantic poet discovers a form
of primordial electricity, a charge to overcome the platitudes of
reason and society. She decides to attune her moral existence to
this natural intensity. The electrical tempest reveals to herself her
own tumultuous moral nature, her true inner identity. Here we
recall Goethe's Werther: 'I felt myself exalted by this overflowing fullness to the perception of the Godhead, and the glorious
forms of an infinite universe became visible to my soul! Stupen-
dous mountains encompassed me, abysses yawned at my feet, and
cataracts fell headlong down before me [. . .]'[11]

   The moral ideal of intensity extended from the nerves of the
body to the storm outside it, and from the individual organism
to the whole of nature. Soon that ideal would also begin to per-
meate technology and culture. In a small 1835 painting of the
Venetian Piazzetta, Turner, who painted so many tempests, snow-
storms, turbulent skies, and torrential rains, explicitly features the
electrical nature of the lightning bolts that always appear to erupt
in his work. In front of the palace of the Doge, a flash of lightning rips through the sky, partially illuminating the dome of St
Mark's and the arcades of the Biblioteca Marciana. Its shape almost
makes it look as if there is an arch of electricity spanning the distance between the column supporting the statue of St Theodore
and the column topped by a towering statue of the winged lion

of St Mark. By a strange coincidence, in the exact same year of 1835, the Scottish inventor James Bowman Lindsay invented the first incandescent electric light bulb. A constant flow of electric charge produced an almost blinding spark between the two poles. The inventor neither protected nor filed a patent for his invention; Edison would commercialise it a few decades later. Above all, Lindsay's bulb did not operate in a vacuum, so it was incapable of perpetuating its illuminating spark indefinitely. But the year that this first primitive light bulb appeared, Turner also painted the storm over Venice like a sort of natural light bulb, prefiguring that future tool that would prove so useful to modernity. In Turner's painting, we see it projected like a fantasy across the landscape of the Doge's city, symbol of classical European culture. One might even say that the columns of St Theodore and St Mark seem to form, *avant la lettre*, the two conductive wires between which the now incandescent filament (here the storm's lightning bolt) lights up. St Mark's Square makes up the base of this gigantic, bizarre light bulb.

The bulb later incorporated a vacuum in an attempt to prolong its durability. But in Turner's brushstrokes, it is as if we can just make out an incandescent light bulb *in the open air*. We might even say that, caught between bourgeois society and the energy of nature, the painting's tempestuous lamp marks the precise threshold separating the end of Romanticism from modernity. Romanticism constantly sought out energy in nature, while for modernity, energy was instead a driving force behind practical and social progress. The electric light bulb is still the same basic storm, but it has been mastered and disciplined. It has been locked up within the confines of a glass dome and forced to light up our cities so that people can continue to move about and work long after nightfall.

We can now summarise the development of our moral model, the intense person. The libertine maintains the electricity of her body's own nervous system, while the romantic uses her nerves to locate the analogue to a macrocosm of tempestuous nature in the microcosm of her own organism. The modern person then captures the storm. She captures lightning in a bottle, puts it in a vacuum, and uses it for technical purposes.

The rocker, electrified adolescent[12]

The electrification of objects brought about a change in the ideal of intensity, and this displaced it from the natural world into the technical world. This is far from being simply anecdotal; to see it, we need only think about the electrification of certain instruments, particularly the guitar.

In jazz orchestras, amid the increasing proliferation of brass instruments, the need for these guitarists to make themselves heard, and therefore the need to find a way of amplifying sound waves, led to a series of experiments, beginning in 1910. Telephone microphones were rigged up to violin, banjo, and, later, guitar necks. But all they managed to capture from the vibrations of the instrument's body was a very weak signal distorted by the resonances naturally produced by the shape of the instrument. In 1931 the first officially recognised electric guitar still had a hollow maple body. However, advances made by Rickenbacker, and subsequent developments by Dobro, Audiovox, Epiphone, and Gibson, quickly allowed for the creation of a purely electric, solid-bodied guitar. George Beauchamp, a lover of Hawaiian music, was still in the process of electrifying acoustic steel guitars when he figured out that resonance and other acoustic properties of sound were actually an obstacle to the very concept of an electric instrument. His 1932 guitar resembled an aluminum frying pan and no longer relied on the old principles of resonance. The guitar was equipped with a microphone made up of two horseshoe-shaped magnets that were surrounded by wires. Those wires were also connected to an additional coil made of six magnets of different polarities. Those magnets could then be used to isolate and capture the vibrations of each of the guitar's strings. All of this also made it possible to increase the volume of the guitar at will.

The American patent office was particularly ill at ease with this technical object, and found it extremely difficult to decide if it was a musical instrument or an electrical device. And the truth is that it was actually both. This *electric instrument* used the current and intensity of electricity to amplify sound, and music belonged to the domain of the electric from then on. Moreover, we might also say that that instrument connected the electricity of our technical tools to the nerves and electricity natural to our bodies. So much so that, after a few decades, the electric guitar became the emblem of the third and final form of intense humanity. Hot on the heels of the libertine and the romantic, we discover the adolescent rocker.

Born of poetry and a direct outgrowth of the romantic poet, the rebellious adolescent is no longer a child but still not yet an adult. The adolescent blossomed in twentieth-century popular culture, especially rock 'n' roll.

The adolescent is first of all a hormonal being powered by desire, rage, and frustration, and what is rock if not the electrification of hormones? Recording music and electrical amplification, particularly with guitars, used sound to communicate an image of violent exaltation, the cry of a pubescent being whose freedom constantly runs into the boundaries staked out by parents, family, and society. The young men or women educated in a consumer society were both free and dissatisfied. But their nerves and the howling storms within them began to resonate with the electrical current, formed and deformed by effects pedals, and resounding through speakers in front of an unruly public. The nerves of the libertine and the storms of the romantic found their technical and industrial culmination in rock 'n' roll, where electricity began to run amok.

Electric rock definitely also has its models of morality. We might think, for instance, of the discouraged narrator in Eddie Cochran's 'Summertime Blues'. Forced to work all summer to make a few bucks, he hopes to call a girl and get a date when the boss tells him, 'No dice, son. You gotta work late.' We see that model when Mick Jagger repeats that he 'can't get no satisfaction', when Roger Daltrey stammers 'I hope I die before I get old', and when Marc Bolan transforms himself into an 'electric warrior'. This moral model is at work when Feargal Sharkey, his voice choked with desire, wants to revel in adolescent pleasure all through the night. Alice Cooper wailed, 'I'm eighteen and I don't know what to say!' Paraphrasing Walt Whitman's poem 'I sing the body electric', Yves Adrien's critical rock manifesto from the 1970s proclaimed, 'I sing the rock electric.' The electric romanticism that Jean-Jacques Schuhl evokes in *Rose poussière* is in part responsible for the birth of rock as a musical genre and as a morality. Rock was a faithful transcription of the hormonal thrashing of puberty, the desire to make love, shout, and bellow, but it was filtered through romantic notions, through spleen and ideal, and fired back in a current of electricity.

This ideal of intense and electric youth showed itself after the Second World War and might have been responsible for the last great modern model of the *fulgurant* person. Fascination with the young rocker indicated a final modern passion. This passion, shared by an ever-larger public, was for a morality consisting of the following: the fast life, the disorderly disturbance of all sensations, the desire to feel the intensities of whatever might happen coursing through you, the impression that the peak of existence is adolescence and puberty, and the feeling that life as an adult is nothing but a series of compromises and resignations, a long, slow depletion of intensity. The model of the rocker is the democratised result of metamorphoses through at least three centuries of a moral ideal. Rock made this ideal available to everybody. Painting with broad strokes, we can say that this ideal had already appeared in the libertine experimentation of eighteenth-century aristocrats. In the nineteenth century, that ideal was extended to the enlightened bourgeoisie with an affinity for Romanticism. Finally, in the twentieth century, it was domesticated, democratised, and incorporated into technology through the use of electric instruments. The intense form of humanity began by maintaining intensities within the body. It then attempted to sustain the intensities of nature as a whole, and ended up democratising them through techniques of amplification, recording, and mechanical dissemination.

From this point of view, the eighteenth-century libertine, the nineteenth-century romantic, and the twentieth-century rocker and adolescent are three models in the same secret history. This history traces how an ideal made it possible to conceive of life as an electric experiment in order to maintain the intensity of the modern world, a world that is always on the brink of collapse in a sort of depression of reason. Beginning in Europe, that ideal became increasingly popular and was soon common throughout most of the West. The libertine, the romantic, and the rocker are three models of the same humanity, one that demands more than lighting, heating, electrical appliances, and the other material benefits brought home by electricity. This kind of humanity lets electricity course through and exalt the whole of its being. The impact of this project on the youth of the twentieth century was extensive. This democratisation had real effects and, for the majority of people, intensity now had to do with the normal way of arranging one's life, not a moral ideal fit only for certain exceptional people. No longer rooted in a singular *morality*, intensity started to be understood in a much more general, *ethical* sense.

Adjectival morality, adverbial ethics

The distinction between morality and ethics can be explained in terms of the grammatical difference between adjectives and adverbs.[13] A moral objective is determined by an adjective, whereas ethical objectives are determined by adverbs. Jacques Brunschwig's formula – cited by Frédérique Ildefonse – applies to stoicism as well as Plato and Aristotle when it claims that 'ethics is adverbial'.[14] The distinctive feature of ethics is to define an adverb indicating how one should live. Conversely, we might say that morality characteristically valorises one or more adjectives that stand for the qualities that we should acquire. Morality calls me to be just, worthy, and respectful. Ethics demands that I act *justly, worthily,* and *respectfully* what I am. We can exercise justice unjustly, and we can be good at doing bad, just as we can be bad at doing good. Ethics is adverbial because it is a question of ways and manners of doing things. It is not concerned with content. On the other hand, morality fixes its values and ideas in place without first worrying about how behaviour might be modified to suit them.

Maybe ethics and morality cannot exist without one another, but this simple distinction lets us understand that the value that people see in themselves either pertains to a way of doing things or to the contents of a thing they do. Ildefonse notes that in most ancient moralities, definitions of the greatest good, virtue, and happiness are expressed through the use of an infinitive modified by an adverb. For example, the purpose is 'to live according to nature'. Ethics enters the scene through this 'according to'. Generally speaking, ethical propositions are systematically applied to ways of doing things and are expressed with an adverb or adverbial locution. This means that the contents of an ethical proposition such as 'act faithfully' can be morally contradictory. A person can faithfully follow an imperative to always tell the truth or to lie to protect someone. She can be equally faithful ethically in both cases, even if her morality isn't the same. Two people can also have the same morality and share identical values but still relate to them differently and act according to oppo- site ethics. We almost always maintain two types of friendships, moral, adjectival friendships and ethical, adverbial ones. We feel an affinity for people who share our ideas, values, tastes, and principles, even if their intelligence and ways of acting, thinking, and living are different. But then we are also friends with other people who have unfamiliar moral or political principles. They might even shock us from time to time, but we see in them our same way of doing things or thinking, and can identify with them ethically. In this case, the way that we relate to our values brings us together even if our particular values pull us apart. There can be no doubt that it's up to each person to decide if they prefer moral or ethical friendships. Every individual has to decide if a relationship is best when based on moral contents or on a way of relating to moral contents, however different they might be.

It seems that intensity began as a servant of *morality*. First the libertine, and then the romantic, searched for a nervous, sentimen- tal, or existential intensity. We then conceived of a sort of exciting moral ideal that everyone based their behaviour on, aimed for, and maintained through love, friendship, and conversation. The enthusiasm that eighteenth-century Europe inherited as a cardi- nal principle of life provided the contents for both eroticism and militant revolutionary zeal. Nevertheless, the concept of intensity can never remain as a content for long. By signifying resistance to identification, intensity is first and foremost a *difference*. When intensity is understood as a relationship, it quickly becomes less of an object and more of a *way* of doing things.

A simple ethics quickly replaced the morality of this intense form of humanity. This ethics could spread far and wide because of its near-total compatibility with other beliefs. Intensity was democratised because it came to be more like an ethical principle than a morality. Of course, the reverse also holds; intensity's moral content became less important than its form because it was democratised and shared by the vast majority. Maybe we couldn't agree on what life was to be, but we could still agree that it should be lived intensely.

Notes

1. From Richard Seaver and Austryn Wainhouse's translation of Sade's *Philosophy in the Bedroom*.
2. This translation is taken with minor revisions from Carolyn Purnell's rendering in *The Sensational Past: How the Enlightenment Changed the Way We Use Our Senses*.
3. This striking image recalls the sadistic group-of-humans musical instruments from Michael Moorcock's *Elric of Melniboné* saga. The instruments, used to provide background music to Melnibonéan banquets, are the result of Elric's countrymen having perfected a medical procedure that allows human vocal chords to be tuned so that their screams produce a tortured chorus of singular notes.
4. This is our translation. See de Condillac, *Traité des sensations*, p. 147.
5. Byron, 'Stanzas Composed During a Thunderstorm'.
6. We have used our own translation of Chateaubriand's *René*.
7. This is from Toru Dutt's translation of Hugo, 'Soleil Couchant', p. 81.
8. Deprun, 'Sade et le rationalism des Lumières', p. 81
9. This is our translation from de Sèze, *Recherches phisiologiques et philosophiques sur la sensibilité ou la vie animale*, pp. 156–7.
10. Our translation, from the second preface to *Lettres sur les écrits et le caractère de Jean-Jacques Rousseau*.
11. Goethe, *The Sorrows of Young Werther: Elective Affinities*, pp. 52–3.
12. *Form and Object*'s Book II, Chapter XV: 'Ages of Life' contains a genealogy of adolescence and how it gradually came to encompass all of Western culture. See also the discussion in the final chapter of Cogburn's *Garcian Meditations*.
13. It is worth clarifying that Garcia is building on Frédérique Ildefonse's work to encourage a novel, possibly revisionary, conception of the difference between 'ethics' and 'morality' here. Analytic philosophers have, unfortunately (if Garcia is correct) heretofore tended to treat the two words as if they were interchangeable.
14. Cited in Ildefonse, *La naissance de la grammaire dans l'Antiquité grecque*, p. 204.

5

An Ethical Ideal

To Live Intensely

Against the bourgeoisification of intensities

As a moral ideal, the intense character of the libertine and the romantic could still be opposed to non-intense things. But as intensity became an ethical ideal for all, even the least intense things could be experimented upon, perceived, and represented through electricity. Now one could exist strongly, even in spite of being weak.

However, the ideal of intensity had long been sustained by its opposition to other models that negated vital intensity. The libertine, the romantic, and the electric adolescent clashed with three contrary models that embodied social norms and the champions of the established order: the priest, the magistrate, and the professor. These counter-models acted as a foil for the intense person and became a constant target for satire in the margins of official culture, in the poems of the bohemians and the whims of the Zutistes.[1] They were mocked in the tracts, pamphlets, and insolent manifestos produced by the Russian and German avant-gardes, as well as in the surrealist and situationist creations. Opposition to the vital non-intensity of the social order provided a charge that electrified the minds of emboldened avant-gardists. This allowed artists and revolutionaries to lash out against predictable ways of living and their failure to sustain the fundamental intensity of the world.

As long as she was connected to a particular moral content, the intense person could be interested in all things save the ennui of people who do not truly live. And let's be even more precise: she can even find ennui interesting, provided that it is a strong ennui, a legendary ennui. It would have to be something akin to the extraordinary neurasthenia of Bartleby and Oblomov, the inactivity staged in the 1960s by the aesthetics of 'incommunicability' in Moravia's novels and Antonioni's films.

The person who feels the weakness of her life's intensity is not necessarily the opposite of the intense person, because even the experience of a weak intensity is susceptible to this intense transmutation. Through an alchemy unique to modernity, it is possible to transform the weak into the strong, the small into the large, inactivity into work, and to create an impression of aesthetic depth in the emptiness of existence. No, the intense person's opposite is above all *weakly weak*, which is to say, average.

The opposite of the intense person is the lukewarm person.

This lukewarmness is almost always a mark of unworthiness in the discourse of lovers, poets, and politicians. The language of joyous exaltation is usually reserved for members of our own side. Our worst enemies merit the use of a vocabulary that is passionate, but also insulting. But only the language of disgust and dishonour can describe those who refuse to choose. Such people are *a little of everything* but *intensely nothing*. In his essay on the subject, Philippe Garnier asks, 'What can be said for that minuscule bit of desire, conviction, and appetite that defines lukewarmness?'[2] Lukewarmness is neutral as well. Scorned for its lack of engagement, it is also a synonym for cowardice. The lukewarm person attempts to straddle the current of history and keep everyone happy without choosing a side. As a neutral party, the lukewarm person is a potential traitor to all sides. She operates by skilfully manoeuvring around contradictions. Such neutral people act as if they have no strong intensity whatsoever. The depletion experienced by the neutral, lukewarm person is a poverty of potential, not a state of purity. She is what she is in a mediocre way.

The mediocrity found in poetry, novels, films, and modern songs has become increasingly remote from the *aurea mediocritas* (the 'golden mean') of which the Latin poet Horace sang. Now mediocrity is more commonly used to designate the irremediable lack that characterises the average person. The average person is 'flat'.[3] Any strong intensity, up to and including suffering, is better than a mediocre truth, a mediocre beauty, or a mediocre life.

Perhaps this conviction should in part be seen as the residue of an aristocratic ethics that persists in democratic times. Instead of judging the content of a behaviour, we now prefer to valorise the excellence of its features and assess its intensity. True nobility is a question of style, not names. Whether you are a fascist, a revolutionary, a conservative, a petty bourgeois, a holy man, a dandy, a man of virtue, a con artist, or a gangster, be it with force. And now we can see the democratic transformation of the term. Rather than being an intense person, what now matters is to intensely be the person you are.

In this sense, the ideal of intensity is flexible enough to incorporate its opposite. More and more often, flatness, neutrality, depression, and mediocrity have been re-established with surprising force. In these cases, the intense person honestly recognises the potential value of mediocrity. From the moment when mediocrity no longer happened mediocrely nor flatness flatly, we could convert them into stimulating experiences. Houellebecq's early novels provide good examples of this. Modernity praised the ability to powerfully evoke the weariness of existence, moments that ring hollow, and low intensities of sensation, belief, and thought. We also find captivating descriptions of this in Chekhov, Carver, and Munro. These works search out the mystery of ordinary life and plumb the emotional depths of existences that appear to have been reduced to little more than a stilled, stagnant surface. And so everything that had once resisted intensity ended up giving way to it, as literature continued its journey through areas that had long been confined to the shadows of everyday democratic existence. Ennui, mediocrity, and provincial life acquired a sort of aesthetic electricity, the lacklustre flamboyance that had already begun to coalesce in Flaubert's novels.

What was then left to resist this aesthetic intensity? Only the social embodiment of the *averagely average*. That embodiment, which would come to mean so much to the modern mind, was given a name: the bourgeois. Simone de Beauvoir summarises the point well in her *Memories of a Dutiful Daughter.* 'Mediocrity is bourgeois.'[4] All those who for a little more than a century had desperately desired intensity as a way of living and thinking hated the bourgeoisie. The bourgeoisie were an intermediary social

class, not an aristocracy safeguarding the past, nor a proletariat
for whom the future seemed to hold so much promise. For the
modern person, to be called 'bourgeois' was the ultimate insult.
And what does it really mean to be called bourgeois? It means:
'You have no intensity.' As in the well-known caricature of Louis-
Philippe in the shape of a pear, the bourgeois has a kind of softness
to it. A bourgeois person is self-satisfied; she eats her fill and then
persists a bit more. Flaubert's Homais is a perfect example of such
a person, and the bourgeoisie are also the target for Rimbaud's sar-
castic barbs. They are on the receiving end of the young people's
insults in Brel's 'Le Bourgeois' ('the bourgeoisie are like pigs') and
the subject of comic mockery in a line from Verlaine's 'Monsieur
Prudhomme': 'He's a happy in-between, a paunchy botanist.'[5]
From Borel to Baudelaire, and from Daumier to Courbet, all the
way to the Mr Jones who finds himself cornered in Dylan's 'Ballad
of a Thin Man', the bourgeois is the person who passively resists
the intensification of her senses. Sitting in the glowing lamplight
of her living room, she is devoid of internal electricity.

  The bourgeois person is settled, sedentary, married, and holds
tight to a cookie cutter plan that guides her life. Security is the primary bourgeois concern. Her mind, which is always strictly delim-
ited and properly formatted, loves to love with moderation, and
knows just enough about science to get by. Bourgeois people such
as merchants or accountants serve as the point atop which society finds its balance. But they are also the final point of resistance
against the ethics of intensity. Paradoxically, the bourgeois resistance
to the ethics of intensity is precisely what makes it possible for that
ethics to be maintained. In the face of bourgeois adversity, the idea
of living intensely regains its transgressive and electrifying meaning. Surpassing even her pedantic peers, the priest and the philosopher, the bourgeois person undoubtedly comes to represent the
last *opposition* to intensity. She has no taste for danger or gambling.
The slightest thrill compels her to double-check that she is still
safe. In bourgeoisification, the soul runs the risk that there might
no longer be any risk at all. Berdyaev declares as much in his 1934
The Destiny of Man: 'Liberation from the fear of eternal damnation
and from all transcendental terrors gave birth to the kingdom of
bourgeois commonplace smugness. [...] Emancipation is a great

blessing, but it brings with it the danger of vulgarising life, of making it flat, shallow, and commonplace.'[6]

But the bourgeois person also wanted to be intensely what she was. She wanted the daily experience of thrills and chills while remaining comfortably planted in her seat. After all, the experiment with Leipzig's kiss was aimed at the bourgeois from the very beginning. The spectacle and consumption of intensities and electric charge were crystallised in the promise of the entertainment industry, nickelodeon, movies, and theme parks. Everywhere you look, there are different products that attempt to convince the working public to part with their money in exchange for feeling alive. The bourgeois resistance, the last moral content to resist the universalisation of the ethics of intensity, thus ceases to function.

We have now been driven back to the beginning of our investigation. We have returned to a description of the condition that we all share in common.

Intensity is no longer identified as a content. Now it just refers to a way of doing things. This means that everyone is free to try to spice up their bland existence. A light electrical impulse can make daily drudgery into a stimulating flurry of activity. This ethical principle has been generalised, and the intense person is thereby forced to invent *ruses* that might allow her to evade the bourgeoisification that constantly threatens her feeling of being alive.

Ruse one: variation

The attempt to thwart the bourgeois normalisation of life consists of interpreting intensity in terms of *variation*.[7] Inverting the classical way of thinking, the intense person discovers that her sensations allow her to understand the passage from one state to another better than something that remains in the same state. In this way, variation can be seen as a principled refusal to submit feeling to a process of domestication. To love the same person exclusively and faithfully seems akin to throwing water on the feeling of love just as it starts to burn brightest. To reawaken and galvanise desire, you have to change, learn to feel a variety of passions, experience all kinds of love, constantly measure what differentiates them, and discover the unknown. The process of forging human experience requires a constant change of object. In this sense, the identical weakens sentiment, while difference strengthens it.

It is necessary to *modulate* experiences in order to keep them from becoming bourgeois. The intense person joins in a race against any way of identifying what she is, knows, or feels. Maybe perception's tendency to concentrate on relationships is the reason why the intense person never perceives the thing itself. The intense person only perceives what distinguishes one thing from another, the invisible hyphen between two moments or beings. What a sentient being is capable of doing only ever reveals itself through contact with another. We unlock the potential of a being's nature by continuously passing from one relation to another. It should also be noted that the intense person tires quickly. She always wants to be someone else. She runs from being bourgeois and, in so doing, falls into boredom. Everything that promises an ideal or definitive form of thought is quickly corrupted, and leaves her with a pressing desire to move on to something else. What doesn't vary may be true, but it's not alive. Things that remain simple, certain, and immutable certainly satisfy the intellect – which is the dead part of the body – but they all end up disgracing the feeling of living within us. This feeling is only ever exalted when manifold. Varying affections are mirrored by music, just as they might be in the flowing water of a fountain or a changing sky. The intense person distrusts thought, knowledge, and language because they all reduce living variation to stable entities or quantities and end up making the world unliveable. The intense person tries out different tricks of thought and searches for an original metaphor to capture what escapes her. To her it seems better to present the mind and perception with a shimmering object, a perpetual variation of being, a sort of movement without mover. The whole point is to combat all forms of establishment and anything else that threatens to petrify the feeling of living, which is why this ruse most often materialises when we compare true life to music. From Romanticism to rock, the musical form brought out the most faithful image possible of that part that dwells within each of our hearts and refuses to be enslaved to language, concept, and immobility. This same ruse appears in Boucourechliev's thought as 'movement without support'.[8] To take up once more Bernard

Sève's analysis in *L'Altération musicale*, music serves as a liberated
ethics since 'nothing in the musical process can stay in place, identical to itself; the simple prolongation of a note in time, *a fortiori* its
identical repetition, already produces difference'.[9]

The modern person was driven by the adverbial ideal of acting, feeling, and thinking in a way that imitated a lightning strike.
She fought to not become bourgeois, and felt no excitement for
anything that a priori stays the same. She lost her taste for identities and could hardly make anything out unless it was variable.
Work routines and actions that could be repeated indefinitely
became intolerable to her. The mere idea of eternity made her
yawn, and marble left her cold. Everything that denies life and its
musical versatility became a source of irritation. To her, perfection
and the absolute came to seem like a defect of being, a weakness in becoming, signalling the destitution of a being's intensity.
After being hooked up to the living ideal of variation, the supreme
object of religious contemplation and the ultimate aims of wisdom come to seem particularly weak to her by comparison. She
likes musical alteration and believes that repetition is like a little
taste of Hell. She feels smothered as soon as she detects any lack
of possibility, and like Kierkegaard's man, she feels condemned to
have to *recognise* what she *knows*. Things that are the same are all
the same to her. She has to have *more* or *less* and prefers unpredictable changes of opinion to established certitudes. Curious about
everything, she can enjoy pain just as much as pleasure. This is
because she loves moments of change and feels the feeling of living as if it were a movement, a sort of melody alternating between
harmony and dissonance.

Ruse two: acceleration

But a way of doing things can quickly turn back into a content,
and all ethics runs the risk of becoming nothing more than a
morality: to do everything in various ways ends up being the same
as doing nothing but *varying*. It is to forever vary in a way that
never changes. Here is a commonplace ethical dilemma: a person
lives for subversion and insolence and finishes up turning trans-
gression itself into a norm. She suddenly finds that she fits into the

bourgeois mould in spite of herself. This vague spectre haunts the intense modern person. That person strives to maintain her own intensity and to prevent it from becoming a norm.

It is thus necessary to invent a new ruse to derail this process of bourgeoisification. Our intense person resists the comfortable establishment of her sensations, but a system of *variation* of intensity alone is not enough for her. She also demands a continuous *increase*. It's not enough for intensities to vary, they must also increase. Everything has to grow increasingly stronger to keep from becoming fixed in place. I get used to the seasonal transition from pain to pleasure, joy to sadness, and darkness to light. It's an established order that is tranquil and reassuring enough for now. There is sunshine after the rain. To resist this familiarisation of intensities, it is absolutely necessary to increase the pain I feel until it strikes me with ever greater force. A growing satisfaction has to course through my body and engulf every part of me. My provocations must become even more shocking, and the idea that guides me must be interpreted in even more radical ways. But it is also necessary for the night to appear darker, for the roar of noise to grow louder, and for me to be possessed more violently by love. Our intense person has to increase all signs and effects of her vitality in the hopes of not becoming mired in a kind of existence, caught up in the entropy of desire. This process of necessarily increasing intensities has no end. This infinite intensification gets mixed up with our own efforts at living and soon makes its way into all of our hopes and dreams. Scientific progress, the march of history, and the development of economic prosperity all serve to motivate the intense person. She knows that she can only maintain intensity if she can make everything faster and livelier. The intense person of libertinism or Romanticism is soon transformed into the exalted sort of person found in the avant-garde, surrealist, futurist, constructivist movements. This intense person brings to the table a manifesto for a new kind of humanity. As Rimbaud wrote, he hopes 'to hold the ground gained'.[10] From one generation to the next, the intense person calls for an advance, a decisive breakthrough, in poetry, thought, the visual arts, politics, and culture. Onward! Constant acceleration at lightning speed in automobiles, trains, and planes carries us far away from the prehistoric and mythical world where repetition was the supreme value of culture. When they grew tired of the old world, poets such as Apollinaire, Marinetti, and Pessoa hoped that modern life would heighten our perceptions and allow us to uproot the old, ordinary ideas and classic works. From this point of view, modernism has a more powerful hold on the mind than any other drug. It promises to pull humanity up out of the depths of banality through an unimaginable, overwhelming form of excitation. Of course, you can build up a tolerance for this drug. But that's okay. All you need is to increase your dosage, and to use thought to accelerate your movement even further.

Baudrillard notes that, after a general survey of history, we can move beyond it in our minds: 'And this change is due to an acceleration: we try to go faster and faster, so well that we have actually already arrived at the end. Virtually! But we are still there.'[11] Theories of the singularity, as well as the accelerationist movement of Nick Srnicek and Alex Williams, all end up repurposing this modernist ruse for their own ends. The modern speed that had once enchanted the poets was no longer enough, and ageing cars seemed to slow to a crawl half a century after leaving the factory. We may be excited by the unparalleled speed of our contemporary vehicles, but we still know that the cars of today will necessarily be slower than those of tomorrow. We're already past the point of no return; we have to go *even faster* than the current maximum speed. The technological singularity is itself a representation of the acceleration of technological progress to a point beyond which a super-intelligent machine will take the place of human intelligence.[12] The 2013 'Manifesto for an Accelerationist Politics'[13] rejects the old Left's timid critiques of neoliberalism and technological progress and defends the acceleration of that progress in terms of progressive political thought. Emancipation isn't about slowing the intensity of progress. We have to use thought to go even faster than progress itself and imagine 'a future that is more modern'.[14] We have to overcome our all-too-familiar way of thinking about acceleration so that it can be felt once again. We must not accept the exhaustion that plagues conservative thinking. We must invent more and emancipate ourselves further. Continuing to progress as before is like treading water; we are soon pulled back into regression and become reactionary. We have to pick up the pace and get *ahead of the curve*. The cost of all progress is that we have to 'accelerate the process of technological evolution'.[15]

Of course, the pleasure we find in acceleration falls under the logic of addiction. What is at stake in the idea of progress is something akin to the increasing feeling of satisfaction brought about by the use of morphine. Thomas de Quincey very early described and analysed this effect of dependency: 'All organisms [...] that have received morphine for a period of time feel the need to receive larger doses: it's a somatic need [...]. We believe that there is no man, no matter how well immersed, well-read, and energetic he may be, who can serve as an exception to this rule.'[16] In 1822 De Quincey calls morphine and opium a 'divine poison'[17] and depicts the paradoxical effects of their use: the delightful feeling decreases even as it is maintained, and can only be maintained by increasing it. Translated by Baudelaire, De Quincey was among the first to sense this paradox: what remains the same shrinks away. After a while, an increase in dosage is merely perceived as static; more is needed to maintain the same sensation. In all perceived progress, the intense person discovers that her thirst for more can only be quenched by a redoubled sort of increase. She has a vague feeling that the more her sensation grows, the harder it becomes to make that growth continue.

In just this way, a third and final ruse comes to mind.

Ruse three: 'primaverism'

As the feeling of progress becomes harder to maintain, the intense person dreams of an experience of the strongest variety, one that would not have to be increased or maintained. As a verse of Paul-Jean Toulet reads, 'It's because it's *the first time*, / Madame, and the best.'[18] In 'Morning of Drunkenness', Rimbaud sings the praises of the first time's supreme power: 'Hurrah for the wonderful work and for the marvelous body, for the first time!'[19] The effect of De Quincey's 'divine poison' decreases as the dosage is increased. Rimbaud writes that the first time is, on the contrary, a 'poison [that] will remain in all our veins even when, the fanfare turning, we shall be given back to the old disharmony'.[20] The

pure promise of every first experience has to give way to repetition, routine, and the erosion of feeling that comes with age.
The fight against bourgeoisification causes the intense person to
treasure innocence, and to think of it as a maximal intensity situated at the very heart of experience. This image gives her some
solace in the face of a kind of progress that proves to be both
addictive and increasingly painful to maintain. Nostalgia is the
balm that soothes the pain of forced progress. But nostalgia is
an old sentiment. To protect herself from the problem of having
to maintain an accelerated level of progress, the intense modern
person invented another ruse that is no less paradoxical for all of
its subtlety. Consciousness developed a taste for innocence and
the kind of intensive experience that thinks that things are most
intense when they are done for the first time.

The rapper Drake asks, 'When was the last time you did some-
thin' for the first time?' This intense person changes, makes progress, and accelerates, but she also keeps track of her first time
trying things and all of her first encounters. She thinks that her
ever more intense experiences still inevitably distance her from
what she felt during their initial moment of impact, when their
intensity was at its strongest. This is the feeling expressed in Rob-
erta Flack's song 'The First Time Ever I Saw Your Face', from
which we take the following couplets: 'The first time ever I kissed
your mouth' and 'The first time ever I lay with you'. Admittedly, at
the end, the singer hopes that this love will last forever, but she also
makes it feel as if the first time can never be surpassed; the passionate memory of the first time breathes life into all of the times to
follow. There is the first time I drank, the first time I smoked, the
first time I loved, the first time I hugged, and the first time I gave
birth ... Of course, the second time makes it possible to increase,
refine, correct, and deepen the feeling of a first experience. But
it is only in the first experience that feeling engages itself *in its
entirety*. Everything that comes along a second time becomes less
intense in this precise sense; only a first experience can still also
be a once-in-a-lifetime experience. No experience can be unique
the second time around.

By combining the Italian word *primavera*, which means 'springtime', and the notion of *verismo*, an aesthetic movement that searched

for the truth in reality, we can arrive at the notion of 'primaverism'. We will use the word 'primaverism' to designate the intense person's tendency to become dissatisfied with variation and progress alone. Primaverism consists of a tendency towards thinking that the greatest truth is only found in childhood, puberty, the first time doing things, and the earliest periods of history. A 'primaverist' believes that deep down nothing is ever stronger than it was at the beginning, and that everything that progresses, grows, and develops does nothing but lose intensity. We can see an example of this primaverism in pop culture's current fetishisation of adolescence as the place where we find the truth of human feeling. Every being has its springtime, a time when the organism wakes up to the life around it and its sensations are at the height of their power. The majority of aesthetic *revivals* and the hope of returning to the songs and sayings of one's youth can be explained in this way. This same principle also allows us to explain modern art's primitivist taste for tribal and outsider art. Primaverism also makes it clear why certain artists, such as Breton, like to throw progress into reverse and always prefer the 'primitive vision' to the lifelessness resulting from the work of consciousness and instrumental reason. Here we can pick out the indirect effects of Rousseau's idea that history puts a distance between us and our most vivid, natural sentiments. The libertines use primaverism in their erotic games. The Marquise de Merteuil enjoys playing with Cécile de Volanges' initial innocence, her 'springtime of feeling' forbidden to the Marquise because of increased consciousness.[21] Lorenzaccio wants 'to see in the 15-year-old child the scoundrel that is to come'.[22] The very picture of innocence contains within it the image of the inescapable corruption of sentiment.

Now we can understand how this final ruse plays out. Rather than being situated in front of us, with an end somewhere out there in the future, the ideal of intensity instead gets displaced into the past, where it persists like a point of origin or dwelling place.

But with time, the three ruses that had made it possible to continue living intensely – through variation, with acceleration, or by clinging to the maximal intensity of the first time (and mourning its loss) – threaten to cancel each other out. The more frenetically things vary, the more difficult it becomes to develop any one idea or feeling in particular. An increase in an idea or feeling only pushes its first occurrence, the moment when it was supposed to be most powerful, further and further away. Thinking that nothing can ever pack as much of a punch as the shock of the first time means having to give up on the notion that there is anything greater to be found in the comparison or variation of our experiences.

The ideal of intensity thus seems to be undermined by an internal contradiction stemming from the different ways of achieving it. Is it really the case that being intensely one way doesn't somehow also make us less intensely another way? The more committed people become to their ruses and the more they defend life's intensities against being identified and neutralised, the more exposed and susceptible those intensities become to identification and neutralisation. Paradoxically, the very act of protecting the intensities of life is what leaves those intensities defenceless. Multiplying intensities is the same as dividing them. To add them is to subtract them, and to increase them is to decrease them. Even their variation is ultimately a kind of uniformity.

At this stage of our inquiry, and in spite of the mystery that surrounds it, the paradox is simple. The ideal of intensity had only just begun to reveal its contradictory character during its days in the minority. But after being generalised, democratised, and made into an adverb, the ideal of intensity could no longer hide this conceptual flaw; whatever reinforces the feeling of life always threatens to weaken it just as much. This exhilarating feeling can only be maintained when we let it overflow; we have to do this, even at the risk of contradicting our initial motivations; we *must* live more and more intensely.

Until the collapse

A norm may be nothing other than an inherited ideal, something that we haven't chosen. The ideal chosen by the intense people of modernity became a value to be imposed upon people in the contemporary world. The fall of most of the world's communist regimes, the globalisation of trade, the miniaturisation and democratisation of telecommunications, and the development of a service economy gave rise to what became the pivotal model for the liberal world. More than intense, this new person was *intensive*. An 'intensive person' is a subject submitted to the *demand* to be intense. She has to learn to juggle all the imaginable ruses, and throws in a bit of variation here, some more acceleration there, and a healthy dash of primaverism to top it all off. She does this in response to a social injunction that demands that she always love, work, and have fun with ever greater intensity. Of course, it is paradoxical to define intensity normatively. After all, intensity is the savage concept of something that cannot be reduced to being. As soon as we take it as a given, it slips right through our fingers. This is precisely why everyone who submits to this norm must reintensify it, recharge it, and restore its violent, uncontrolled character. They must not treat it as a given. They need to have norms, but they don't want to conform; they have to choose their own norms. They are confronted with a contradictory task.

Once normalised, intensity invaded the social world and served as a measure of the free actions of individuals. Having been quantified, calculated, and subjected to statistical analysis, intensity came to look like its own opposite. Intensity once embraced everything that escaped conceptualisation, but now it was used to complete the rationalist conquest of the social world. Paradoxically, intensity was now used to cut up all the dynamics, energies, and everything else that escaped from rationalism into numbers and figures that could be evaluated, deciphered, and compared. The terms that defined the modern, intense person have thus been reversed in the case of the contemporary, intensive person. The assertion of intensity over extension, quantity, and number creates an extensive, quantifiable, and countable kind of intensity.

Consider this example from the world of sport. Recent history clearly demonstrates the emergence of a model intense person, and soon thereafter, the rise of a model intensive person, all of which culminates with the challenging of norms in the name of an ideal. Modern sports were born from the idea of a new person, one who appeared to revive the Greek Olympic ideal, but whose true destiny would be to intensify and put on display all of the possibilities of the human body. The codification of individual and team sports in the nineteenth century had less to do with reviving the lost rituals of an ancient civilisation, and was instead more focused

on celebrating the modern maximisation of all of humanity's functions and abilities. The preacher Henri Didon's famous saying 'citius,
altius, fortius', 'faster, higher, stronger', was taken up by the Baron
de Coubertin in the Olympic motto, and it is a perfect summa-
tion of the ideal of intensification that we are aiming for. Dressed
in the trappings of ancient culture (for example, the use of Latin),
the Olympic motto captures the desire to measure and push the
boundaries of our performance as far as possible in every direction.
It speaks of the organism as if it were a reservoir of energy capable of
generating speed, force, and explosive muscular activity. The usage
of the comparative form of 'strong' (fortius) in the Latin expression
is evidence of the victory of intensive imagination over extensive
imagination. In the first instance, modern sport is grounded in an
ideal of the body, one which is an idealisation of the pure physical
energy of humanity. Sport is supposed to let everyone come to an
understanding of their being, as well as vary and enhance it. Sport
should be more about participation than winning.

But we can now quickly detect what was an almost imperceptible slippage of intensity from ideal to norm. The systematic
comparison of performance, and specifically the measurement of
performance itself, soon became more important than the cel-
ebration of the human body's energy. Starting in the 1930s, an
increasing amount of attention was focused on keeping track
of records, and new developments in the measurement of time
allowed for more and more minute differences between runners
to be measured. Electronic timekeeping even made it possible to
discern minuscule segments of time that had hitherto been invisible to the naked eye. We ask athletes to repeatedly perform the
same movements in order to intensify them. Most importantly, we
want to measure their movements and establish a kind of exact science of performance. Training in all fields follows this same logic;
we see it in different techniques for dieting and recovery and in
the constant deployment of huge batteries of statistics. Little by
little, the ideal of intensity became a norm, and we passed from
the modern person to the person born of the liberal world, from
the athlete to the performing individual. The potential for setting
personal records is at once endless and limited by the physiology
of the human body. There is a marked decline in new records set

in athletics. Swimming had to turn to controversial methods such as polyurethane material blends for swimwear and doping to find its second wind, and, for years now, we have been able to see how much of a problem medical and technological one-upmanship has been in cycling.

And then a third and final moment comes along. The intensivist norm breaks with the ideal of intensity, so the intensive person creates different ruses in an attempt to give athletic intensity back the power that it once had. How can this be done? By going beyond the rules and putting some skin back into the game. From this perspective, we can understand the popularisation of non-traditional, 'extreme' sports: base jumping, bungee jumping, gliding, ski jumping, and skydiving, as well as the high dive and freediving. In their article 'Jouer avec la gravité' ['Playing with gravity'], sociologists Guillaume Rotier and Bastien Soulé note the following:

> Many observers of contemporary athletics emphasise the radicalisation and heightened frequency of exposure to danger. People have tried to explain this phenomenon by approaching it from many different angles; it has been thought of as a product of the search for strong sensations, a way of answering the call of the wild or breaking the routine of the everyday, or as an affirmation of one's identity, and so on.[23]

The old intensities have been regulated and quantified; they are neutralised, shoved into the mould of bourgeois conformity, and reduced to being norms. With time, the intensive person becomes doomed to invent increasingly risky and *extreme* kinds of sports in order to feel alive.

From the evolution of pornography to the maximisation of physical performance through steroid-fuelled body-building, up to and including cocaine use and self-harming (as Trent Reznor sang, 'I hurt myself today / To see if I still feel'), it is no longer possible to pretend that all of modernity's apparent perversions were confined to the seamy underbelly of liberal society. Today those same perversions instead look as if they were scrupulously modelled in accordance with the modern ideal of intensity. There is a constant struggle to rescue intensities from the norms of society. Caught in a perpetual race against the social normalisation of intensities, the intensive person redoubles her own intensity. Variation becomes frenetic, and acceleration becomes hyperbolic. And the feeling that the intensity of life is shrinking and growing more remote takes on a pathological form and becomes depression.

The individual in liberal society must contend with two thoughts that stand in open contradiction. They feel as if all things must be intensified, but at the same time they know that the task itself is impossible. To achieve it would require us to transcend infinity and act beyond our own intellectual and psychological limits. In this way, the individual in liberal society inevitably arrives at an impasse. To be sustainable, intensity is condemned to being a kind of hyperbolic increase. But looking forward to feeling something stronger than what we feel in the moment makes it more difficult to get a strong feeling in that same moment. If we look at examples of consumption, sexuality, athletic performance, or addiction, we see that a superabundance of intensity also seems to provoke a decrease in intensity. Nicolas Floury shows in his *Ontologie du sujet toxicomane* [*The Ontology of the Addicted Subject*] how the 'addict subject' gets caught in the logic of her own ritual. She repeats the intensity of enjoyment until she is no longer able to enjoy anything but repetition itself.

The only way a living intensity can increase is by *increasing its own increase*. The first pages of Mehdi Belhaj Kacem's *Algèbre de la tragédie* [*The Algebra of Tragedy*] describe this logic, which we might call the 'hystericisation' of the feeling of intensity. When this hystericisation is no longer possible, the individual can no longer keep up the intensification of all the intensities that she perceives and that are demanded of her performance. The result – she collapses. Contemporary philosophy and sociology have thoroughly studied the symptoms of this collapse. This pathology has been given many names, such as 'burnout', exhaustion, or having a breakdown. Jonathan Crary, for example, warns of a new form of capitalism that goes to war with sleep in order to promote the ideal of a life without breaks.[24] According to this ideal, life should be ceaseless activity throughout all hours of the day and night, until we reach a state of global insomnia. We see the image of the 'Burnout Society' that Byung-chul Han describes. There are some who criticise the norms of liberal society, arguing that it demands that individuals must govern themselves in a way that forces subjects into increasingly intensive ways of life until a total breakdown becomes the only possible result. We are sentenced to adapt to an unstable, provisional, and intense world, a world that psychoanalyst Alain Ehrenberg describes as being 'in a permanent state of flux, where everything is changing before [our] eyes'.[25] People can no longer live up to the pressure of maintaining stronger and stronger intensities because it pushes them to the breaking point. What we have here is not the Stakhanovite obligation to be a productive worker. The new mission demands that we sustain intensities that have to be increased in order to be maintained. Pascal Chabot recalls that the term 'burnout' originally referred to the state of an addict 'strung out by using hard drugs too intensely'. Psychotherapist Herbert Freudenberger used this term to describe his own state of fatigue, and the word eventually came to refer to emotional exhaustion and the feeling of inefficiency felt by workers who cannot keep up the pace. Chabot explains that the performance demanded of individuals is endless, and that, for that very reason, people necessarily lose sight of their own self-actualisation.

The demand that life be intensified provokes a kind of discouragement, with well-documented psychological and social effects. That, however, is beyond the scope of our investigation. We want to know how and why it is that *the more intensely we are, the less so we end up being*. We know how to recognise the symptoms of collapse, but the logic behind it is still hazy. Up until now we were content to note that the different ways of living intensely and the various ruses used to maintain the intensities of life end up contradicting each other. But this approach now comes up short. It cannot account for how an individual who relies exclusively on variation, acceleration, or primaverism still collapses in the end. A person in search of nothing but progress, and who regrets nothing, will nevertheless feel a sort of resistance within himself, the early stages of a fatal depletion of feeling. Every time we approach intensity to the exclusion of everything else, we seem to encounter a mysterious principle: whenever an intensity is reinforced, it is equally weakened. What could this secret logic be? Here we are adopting an ethical vantage point, not a moral one, so for now we will avoid getting bogged down in *moral* arguments against the intensivism of liberal society. Instead, we will try to discover the destructive concept at work in all feelings of intensity.

Notes

1. The Zutistes were a group of poets and artists who gathered in the late 1860s and early 1870s. Rimbaud and Verlaine featured most prominently among them. They were infamous for irreverent writing and behaviour (such as swearing, relieving themselves in inappropriate places, and so on) in the service of distancing themselves from the bourgeoisie. One of Rimbaud's most famous lines of poetry, from *A Season in Hell*, emphasises this necessity to change: 'One must be absolutely modern.' Rimbaud, *A Season in Hell*, p. 89. In these respects, Rimbaud is a nearly perfect example of Garcia's angsty adolescent, one who is in fact preserved forever as such because he stopped writing at an early age and then removed himself from the Parisian scene to enter the coffee trade in Abyssinia. And then he died. In this he remains the prototype of the romanticised dead American rock star (for example, Jim Morrison, Kurt Cobain, and so on) who never matures, compromises, converts, or 'sells out'.
2. Garnier, *La tiédeur*, p. 1.
3. It is worth thinking about the connection between the sense of 'flatness' in such passages and the 'flat ontology' of Book I of Garcia's *Form and Object*, which contains a sophisticated account of numerosity, the only quantity to be found in Book I. This lack of qualitative gradations, along with the refusal to ontologically privilege human beings and their psychic and cultural eructations, constitutes one of the two senses of 'flatness' in *Form and Object*. It would be untoward for Garcia to say as much, but surely *some* of the opposition to flat ontology among recent continental philosophers is due to the cultural pathologies that he goes on to convincingly expose in this chapter. See especially the manner in which Garcia's discussion of 'accelerationism' is embedded in his discussion of ruses on page 88.
4. This appears to be Garcia's paraphrase of de Beauvoir, *Mémoires d'une jeune fille rangée*, p. 247.
5. Our translation of Verlaine, *Poèmes saturniens*, p. 44.

6. Berdyaev, *The Destiny of Man*, p. 179.
7. Especially given the uses of 'norm' and its cognates in analytic philosophy, it is very important to be clear about how Garcia marks the distinction between a norm and an ideal in this chapter. For Garcia, an ideal is a standard (for example, perfect honesty). Endorsing an ideal means endorsing the idea that people *should* strive to achieve it, balanced with the expectation that people will not fully succeed in doing so. For Garcia, however, a norm is a combination of what analytic philosophers would describe as both statistically and genuinely normative. A Garcian norm is statistical in the sense that it describes a pattern of behaviour in society that is sufficiently robust for an understanding of the norm to allow one to predict what members of the society will in fact do. But Garcian norms are also genuinely normative (at least for the people in the group subject to the norm) in the sense that the expectation that a norm will be followed is not merely predictive. If people do not follow the norm they are also in some sense perceived to be getting it wrong. The paradox of adolescence lies in the manner in which the wilful violation of norms (in Garcia's sense) itself becomes normative. And Garcia is correct, for what could be more bourgeois at this point in history than trying to shock the bourgeoisie? Donald Trump's appeal to wide swaths of Middle America shows that, like epistemic relativism, this phenomenon is no longer the sole province of people with leftist political and artistic inclinations.
8. See the discussion of Boucourechliev in Sève, *L'Altération musicale: Ou ce que la musique apprend au philosophe*, p. 322.
9. Sève, *L'Altération musicale*, p. 321.
10. Rimbaud, *A Season in Hell*, p. 89
11. Baudrillard, 'Entretien réalisé par Raphaël Bessis et Lucas Degryse'.
12. For Garcia's critique of the cult of singularity, see *Form and Object*, Book II, Chapter VI: 'Humans'.
13. In addition to Williams and Srnicek's '#ACCELERATE MANIFESTO', see Cogburn's satirical '#DECELERATE MANIFESTO'.
14. Williams and Srnicek, '#ACCELERATE MANIFESTO: for an Accelerationist Politics'.
15. Williams and Srnicek, '#ACCELERATE MANIFESTO: for an Accelerationist Politics'.
16. This citation seems to be taken from Arvède Barine's discussion of Thomas De Quincey. See Barine, 'Essais de Littérature Pathologique', p. 141. The quoted passage itself is originally from Georges Pichon's treatise on morphinomania. See Pichon, *Le morphinisme*, p. 4.

17. This citation is taken from De Quincey, *Coleridge and Opium-Eating and Other Writings*, p. 110.

18. This citation is taken from poem XXI of Toulet, *Les Contrerimes: poèmes*, p. 29.

19. Rimbaud, *Illuminations, and Other Prose Poems*, p. 41.

20. Rimbaud, *Illuminations, and Other Prose Poems*, p. 41.

21. de Laclos, Les Liaisons dangereuses.

22. de Musset, *Lorenzaccio*, p. 4.

23. Routier and Soulé, 'Jouer avec la gravité: approche sociologique plurielle de l'engagement dans des sports dangereux'.

24. Crary, *24/7*, p. 8.

25. Ehrenberg, *The Weariness of the Self*, p. 114.

6

An Opposing Concept

The Effect of Routine

There is a logic of intensity

The concept of intensity represents something that resists all logic and calculation. Nevertheless, there is a logic of intensity. This logic explains how and why a living organism or community that exclusively relies on the search for intensity to guide and determine its actions gets itself dragged into a process that is beyond its comprehension. The only way out of the logic of intensity leads to a devastating paradox of modern ethics. The triumph of the intense in all things also indicates its impending defeat. Paradoxically, the more intensity our feelings gain, the more intensity they lose. *Affirming* the intense through thought ends up simultaneously *negating* it. And so we are left with the fact that this division causes intensity to cancel itself out. This same scene is played out on the world stage and in the theatre of emotion within every individual. We see it in the intimate life of people who are constantly exhausted and seem as if they are always on the verge of a nervous breakdown. On the great stage of world culture, modern minds are likewise obliged to watch helplessly as the values that embodied the grand electric promise of the eighteenth century continue their decline.

This paradoxical logic of intensity is not driven by our *reason* but by our *feeling* of being alive. This logic seems to have made its philosophical debut alongside English empiricism, which degraded our impressions, making them less vivid. This system caused the light to fade from our ideas through an endless process of identification and re-identification performed by our perceptive apparatus. But this is the destiny of every sentient being; *habit* itself provokes a slow erosion of emotion in all living things. Experience lets us make sense of life, at least inasmuch as we are living, feeling organisms. And experience presupposes repetition. And repetition necessarily affects all that is perceived with the coefficient of intensity.

This effect is the first principle of life inasmuch as life is thought, and of thought inasmuch as thought is lived. Because they perceive, remember, and identify things, living beings are cut through by violent intensities. Those intensities rush through them and inevitably wear them down by attacking and corroding all liveliness of feeling. All living experience begins to lose intensity as soon as we start thinking about it.

For this reason, we can never demand that our existence or social norms must be 'the most intense possible' without surrendering them to a merciless logic that makes our feelings decrease as our experience is increased. To see why this happens, we have to go back to the source of all lived intensity, sensate experience. It once appeared to us that all intensity had to be *experienced* in order to be maintained. And to live is to maintain intensities in precisely this sense. However, some intensities (such as waves, for example) exist on their own in the inorganic universe. This being said, they are only communicated to the living when they are experienced and perceived. Seeing a colour or hearing a sound transforms the variable intensity (of a wave) into a felt quality. We can think of this felt quality as a *sustained intensity*, an intensity that only exists for and by the organism that perceives it. Instead of remaining as a simple quality (such as wavelength variation) in the objective world, physical intensity instead moved into the subjective world of perception and became something that could be felt, repeated, and redoubled, such as a colour or a sound. The objective intensity of a wave is taken up and maintained by intensifying it through perception. Perception may start out as an electrical impulse, but what is perceived is no longer reducible to quantifiable electrical pulses coursing through the nerves of a living organism. For the subject, there is a feeling of the redness of red, of the silence of silence, and of the hardness of the hard. A sustained intensity is a sort of *intensity of an intensity*. And this is exactly the feeling of a living subject. There are quantifiable intensities that serve as the initial objects of our perception, and then there is the intensity of those intensities, a second kind of intensity that pertains to the qualities that perception attaches to objects. The blue of the sky that I behold as it grows ever more blue is no longer just a wavelength of light being perceived; that blue also becomes an intensity that perception redoubles and sustains throughout time.

The whole drama of the intense person is grounded in the mundane observation that we have to mix thought with sensation in order to sustain intensity. But that is also precisely what ends up cancelling intensity out.

In everything that varies, something remains the same

I hear a piece of music, and out of nowhere I'm surprised by an unexpected change of tuning, key, or rhythm. This variation might shake my ear out of its unfeeling slumber, a numbness brought on by what were all-too-predictable changes in the music at hand. Now I get the feeling that the piece is being played and was composed by someone fed up with rigid bar structures, someone interested in and excited by alterations, breakdowns, and imbalances. I barely have time to grasp the first change before it changes again. This is the case for music with an asymmetrical structure, as is found in some songs from the Balkans. It is the same with improvised music, free jazz, Frank Zappa's compositions, and different forms of experimental metal. Practitioners of such forms think that having to reiterate music is like being trapped in a cage made of sound. They try to escape from repetition and use variation to chase after intensity. As in every ethics of variation, it's all about adopting different ruses to pre-empt perception, playing with norms generated alongside the action of perception, and celebrating the creative character of life while struggling to keep everything from always coming back as the same thing. It is now indispensable never to be where you are expected, to refuse to play any note or chord that could reasonably follow from the preceding one, to adopt a view in opposition to the system, to take the road less travelled, to get off the beaten path, and to give the melodic line or the rhythmic pattern a little twist. And why? All of this is a way of making it known that what is intense in life is that which does not stay identical, that which eludes systematic re-identification, and that which is free to become what it is. Improvised music accomplishes an ethical act every time it changes in an unexpected way in order to avoid being predictable. What improvised music achieves in the order of harmony and rhythm is analogous to the decisions that the intense person makes while always trying to vary, to reinvent herself, and to never get caught in the trap of a predetermined destiny.

And now I think I finally get it. But then I listen to that piece again, and I'm waiting for another surprise. Sure enough, its rhythm and cadence vary once more, as if to express the nervous energy of a person standing in adamant opposition to all rules. This variation is reminiscent of a person who only gets fulfilment in the moments when she manages to step outside of the routine and break with the programme that she has already begun to follow a little too mechanically. And then the tune takes a different tack, and I find myself less and less surprised. From then on, I realise that change itself is precisely what never changes. We can only be certain of irregularity. It's like hanging out with a hipster. They are surprising and captivating in the beginning; however, once you understand that they will never stop flip-flopping from one opinion to another, you start to detect a sort of routine familiarity underlying their unpredictable strangeness. And so it is with the strange unpredictability of the tune now ringing in my ears. Nevertheless, there is still one option left to hipsters, those who play extreme forms of music, and others of their ilk. As soon as I start to see the regularity behind their irregularity, I cannot help but be surprised by a new-found predictability. But now, after metamorphosing and jumping from breakdown to breakdown, what if the music were to halt its transformation and take on an unalterable unchanging time and rhythm? Well, my predictions would be totally derailed. And what if the person who was never the same each time we met and whom I had wound up seeing as an incorrigible hipster definitively established and regulated her behaviour? Then they would have fooled me twice. But they won't fool me again because both the music and the listeners who love it for its perpetual variations of intensity have to face up to the same dilemma. They can either continue to change and institute a sort of permanence of the impermanent, or they can stop changing. The latter option might let them break with habit and routine, but they will have to pay the price and fix themselves in place.

Change can obviously happen in an infinite number of ways. Music can explore these possibilities and can make a listener feel all the subtleties of sequence, series, recursive effects, and even previously unheard-of levels of disharmony. With its capacity for conceptualising all kinds of sequences and its ability to use the natural numbers to index the elements of a series, mathematics makes it possible to generate a formal model of what we might call the *intelligence of change*. We can *conceptualise* variety as the wealth of ways in which the very being of things may vary.

But although abstract thought lets us conceptualise things in terms of such complex and refined logics of change, there is still another, much more rudimentary logic that persists in the background. It is the logic of feeling, and getting rid of it is far more difficult. Rather than worrying about the particulars of a process of change, this obstinate logic only cares about 'whether something is changing or not'. It manages to distil this basic feeling, one that explains our weariness, out of whatever phenomena we might encounter. Once we are confronted with a variation, something in us focuses on the change while overlooking the dazzling impact of that first encounter. This faculty misses the impact of the moment because it already recognises that change itself is an invariable constant. It is content to simply observe that 'something hasn't stopped becoming different'. And it stabilises this idea of variation for feeling.

This faculty has no interest in the subtle ways in which the contents of a thing might change. It is solely focused on accounting for the form of change itself. It corresponds to that thing in every being that perceives and pays attention to the change – or lack thereof – of change, to the variation – or lack thereof – of variation, and to the difference – or lack thereof – of difference. This faculty redoubles the process of becoming, turns it against itself, and ends up shaping feeling in a determinate way. We can also see this same rudimentary logic at work in perception, in the case of the logic of the *routine*.

Routine is powered by a disarmingly simple mechanism that we find nestled in the heart of all of the intensities that we perceive. This mechanism works against our intensities at all times. It's the reason why we end up bored by a tune, even though the music never stops changing. It's also why something in us cannot help being tired of a piece of music despite it constantly inventing and reinventing new ways to surprise us. This very same mechanism is also to blame when we grow numb to even the most effective antics of the very same people who used to reliably shock us day after day. We can always maintain a modicum of interest if someone or something is always changing and is constantly reinvented. However, over time, at least a part of our perception becomes indifferent to astonishment, and is no longer taken aback by the same things that used to shock and amaze it. From that point on, this part of us considers all novelty, and indeed, all *modernity*, as a sort of tradition. It's this part of us that submits to the logic of routine. And despite all of our ethical efforts, our fight to eliminate the logic of routine can only ever partially succeed because the mechanism that powers the logic of routine is also what allows us to identify intensities.

Routine is nothing other than the price to pay for the very possibility of feeling and thinking our intensities.[1] It is the necessary counterpart to *feeling*. Our very attempts to hold back the menace of routine end up making it impossible to experience intensities and sustain them through time.

In everything that increases, something decreases

So now we are caught in a trap. We cannot respond to the routine of variation by continuing to vary or by varying differently, because routine is incompatible with *different ways* of doing things. It only cares about the form of a phenomenon. In the end, it matters little how something changes (that is a concern for an *understanding* of habit). The only thing that matters is whether something changes or not (and that concerns a *feeling* of habit). To extract ourselves from the routine of variation, we then have to rely on a ruse already honed by the intensive person; when musical modulation and other forms of variation no longer suffice, the intensive person goes further and tries to increase and accelerate these intensities. She eventually finds out that the constant variation of pleasures, forms, rhythms, and experiences can no longer help her to maintain any intensity whatsoever. Then there is nothing left for her to do but to accentuate the same perceptions, and to try to revive the same feelings of joy or pain, the same colours and motifs, and the same looping rhythms over and over, with ever greater strength. Our sensations have to be accelerated and deepened if we are to have any hope of overcoming the logic of routine.

Initially, the charade seems to pay off. By no longer aiming for variation, the desire for intensity changes in appearance. I no longer have any fear of repetition; on the contrary, I now earnestly call out for it. I'm not necessarily looking for the return of the same; I just want to try to make room for the progress of a perception or an idea. I want perceptions and ideas to be able to develop and grow in strength; I want to make them more vivid, faster, and more exact. And I freely give myself over to this operation without imposing my expectations as to where this increase might end up. By all appearances, routine is not a problem for things that increase, because routine already seems to play an integral part in reinforcing our feelings and actions. Routine is likewise at work in trance and meditative states and other mental and physical disciplines that require us to repeat the same exercises. Ideas also follow the logic of routine as they progress through history. If, for example, I consider the struggle for the ideals of liberty, emancipation, and human equality, I normally imagine the unflagging repetition of the same demands, year in and year out, generation after generation. I soon picture the painful process by which the liberty and autonomy of individuals come to be intensified by degrees, and I recall the price paid in combat and sacrifice on a long road paved with political victories and defeats. This is why the most repetitive minimalist music no longer manages to evoke intensity through the use of variation. It instead fosters an intense growth of feeling through the obstinate repetition of the same little musical phrase.[2] The effects that this generates make it seem possible to hear the same thing over and over, but in a way that becomes better and more precise each time. Indeed, this is the very same idea behind all notions of progress; progress happens when things are allowed to become what they are a little more each day. Progress means accommodating a process in which things develop, with the stubborn air of someone hammering their truth home.

Increasing intensity is the only way of dealing with the problems that stem from having understood our routine interactions with intensities in terms of pure variation. And even then, the notion of a feeling of intensity exalted by a concept of progress soon proves to be temporary as well. Routine returns again, this time in a slightly different form, to gnaw away at and corrode the very possibility that there could be anything like an infinite increase or growth. Critics of historical progress such as Herder have all insisted that the price to be paid is that the progress of any particular idea through history is always matched by the regression of another idea. For Herder, the 'principle of compensation' is symbolised by the image of sailors who must cast all extra weight overboard so that their ship can continue on its course. It is evident that humanity cannot be the subject of universal history *without a counterpart*. Every time humanity manages to jump ahead and get a leg up on the future, it ends up leaving one of its ideas trailing behind in the past. According to Herder, the extreme intellectualism of the moderns brought about progress in reason, but it also provoked a loss of spontaneous vitality. To him, Egypt and the East give us an image of the childhood of humanity, while ancient Greece paints a picture of humanity's adolescence. Greece therefore gains a certain aestheticisation of existence, a cult of good looks, but it loses the childlike mystery and enigma of earlier times. And likewise, adulthood means that we have to sacrifice spontaneity in order to gain awareness. The more we feel as if we have mastered a feeling or gesture, the more a little something of the original feeling or gesture gets left behind.

Of course, one could argue that *true* progress consists of the intensification of that which is good or desirable and the de-intensification of that which is bad or undesirable. But such a conception implies that the ethical principle of intensification must again be replaced with a value, a moral content; a move in this direction ends up as an argument about morality. The problem is that our modern adverbial ethics valorise all changes of

intensification in exclusively formal terms; no attention is paid
to the specific contents that undergo that process of change. And
when it comes to the construction and maintenance of this kind
of adverbial ethics, arguments from morality soon prove to be
futile. When it comes to intensities, nothing progresses without
making something else regress to the same degree. Absolute progress is not possible for an intensity. What we have instead is a
logic that might be described as 'routine progress'. It is certainly
possible for us to imagine something like an indefinite progress
towards the good, and this might even motivate us to work stead-
fastly towards that end, but there will always be something within
us that resists, unconvinced by this vision of life. When we come
face to face with accelerated progress and the prospect of loss or
ineluctable separation that accompanies it, we experience a dull
feeling that never fails to make a sort of fatigue and despondency
well up within us. This happens for two obvious reasons: first,
the predictability of an increase of intensity itself creates a lack of
excitement about what is to come; moreover, any increase in the
intensity of the states we experience also imposes an increasing
distance between us and our first experiences.

What is it that, over time, always slows the feeling of acceleration? As soon as we think that something (a pleasure or an idea) is
destined to accelerate forever, we imagine its future trajectory and
compare it with its current state of increase. This projection allows
us to inhabit what is known in grammar as the future perfect,
and from that point of view the original state of acceleration will
always have been less than all future states of acceleration of the
same thing. For example, the more we promise economic growth
or technological progress to a society, the more its members are
able to visualise this progress and picture in advance what a richer
or more technologically advanced society would be like. But this
newfound perspective also backfires, and the present state of society or technology comes to be seen as a disappointment. In the
beginning, depictions of progress are exciting and encourage us to
improve, perfect, and enrich what we already have at our disposal.
But we can only maintain progress by getting ahead of progress
itself, and its potential for acceleration seems limitless. What we
now think of as the society and the tools of the future may make

our contemporary world look dated and imperfect, but that same future society and those same tools will look just as obsolete as ours do now from the perspective of another world even further in the future. Our thinking pushes us to make constant progress, but at the very same time something in our feelings becomes less sincere in its enthusiasm. And if we ask just what this something is, we get the same answer as before. It is something that haunts our perception of progress, a thing controlled by the mindless, inexorable logic of routine.

This routine of increase and progress is not solely a product of the fact that all progressions are foreseeable. What matters more is the foundational relationship that such a routine bears to the notion of something that seems to regress to the same degree that it progresses. We could give the intense person everything she could want in her quest to endlessly strengthen all that she perceives and desires. We can even try to imagine what absolute progress might look like. But even if we succeed in all that, we still end up losing the feeling of the first time. Our experiences are reinforced, but the lifeblood is drained from our innocence.

There are fewer and fewer first times

So it looks like primaverism may be our last resort.

Routine destroys feelings of variation and feelings of progress, but it cannot lay a hand on the superior intensity of the first time; memory conserves that intensity. Even better, the effects of routine on the freshness of an experience can be turned against themselves by the very idea that to each particular moment of life there belongs something singular. Even with one foot in the grave, I am still reminded that I am about to experience something unique and unprecedented. I'm going to die *for the very first time*. As an intensive person, I am a devotee in the cult of the *prima volta*.[3] My devotion allows me to defy the inevitability of routine by making the most of the novelty offered to me at every moment. There is nothing keeping us from reframing every repeat experience, and thinking of it as if it were completely new. In this way, someone loving for the second time is also experiencing love for the second time *for the first time*. Once we become aware of them, even routines can become a source of new life experiences. And we might even go one step further and define adulthood as *the part of life when we learn for the first time to stop experiencing the world for the first time*; and yet we somehow still manage to squeeze a little intensity out of that understanding of adult life. The force of the first time seems superior to the effects of routine. After all, when a living being fails to perceive even the slightest novelty, that failure can itself be perceived as something novel. Ennui, ordinary things, and the everyday things that we have already mentioned, up to and including routine itself, can provide us with an intense experience as long as we are doing them for the first time. Nevertheless, soon the everyday will return to feeling like just another day, and the effects of routine will start to kill the intense character of lived experience all over again. Any person who enjoys the singularity of life's every instant is always in danger of succumbing to a bourgeois ethics. Already feeling for the second or third time the familiar pleasure of performing a given gesture for the second or third time, this person becomes habituated, accustomed to being comfortably numb. And even if they don't admit it, their feeling of existing gets a little weaker.

The feeling of innocence is left with one last move. I can try to cut routine off entirely by committing to living every moment 'as if for the first time'. So I decide that I have to make this effort, and I assign myself the task of trying to find the intensity of a first experience in even my most insignificant activities. I try to do everything as if it were for the first time: falling asleep, waking up, every step that I take, every bite that I chew, the moment when I feel the rain begin to fall, and the precise instant when it stops. And then I still have to make an effort to find an intelligent way to instill each sentence spoken, each step taken, and each passing encounter with the excitement of the unprecedented. I play at being an overgrown child, eternally adolescent. I pretend always to be amazed and delighted, and act as if I've never been jaded. I try to preserve the intensity of life by living day after day with the spontaneity of a lover in her youth.

But no matter what I do, it seems that the effects of routine set in again and dull my attempts at spontaneity. *The second time* will be thrust upon me all too soon, and I will have to force myself to act

again 'as if for the first time'. And after all that, I'll still run right back
into the same dilemma regarding the variation of existence. On the
one hand, I can continue to try to do everything as if it were for the
first time; 'doing everything for the first time' would then become
the invariable rule of my existence. But, even if it is only unconsciously, this posture would also begin to wear on both myself and
others. Everyone knows me as naivety's spokesperson. On the other
hand, I can also make this moment the first time that I want to stop
living as if it is the first time. I can familiarise myself with the cosy
charms of a well-domesticated life of habit and perhaps even try to
deepen and increase my very first sentiments. But here again, with
the passage of time, I will inevitably fall back under the sway of routine progress. Whether it be with regard to the maximal intensity of
innocence, or to primaverism as a whole, the effects of routine work
to dull our feeling of intensity. It seems as if there are countless first
times to be had in life, if only because of the little bit of something
unique that belongs to each of our experiences. However, now we
can hear in our minds that the fateful bells have already been set
in motion; their ominous tolling never fails to signal the imminent
decline of feeling. Our first experiences in life keep their distance
from our feelings, in the same way that the exponent of a number is
always at a distance from its base.

Now let's go back to the musical metaphor. I hear the same piece
for the second time. The first time, the experience was unique. This
time, the repeated experience feeds off the first; it might get a little more refined; it might even increase in some way, but it always
ends up pushing me further away from the shock of the original
experience. The experience can still be intense during this second
listening because it's the first time that I am *re-listening* to this piece.
I look forward to paying special attention to details that I might
have previously missed. My experience is enriched at the same
time that the force of the experience loses some of its immediacy.
And then I listen to the piece for a third time. Now I can relate
my first re-listening to this second re-listening in a way that sup-
plements, amends, and corrects it. Each time the feeling will be less
vivid, but also more exact. At this point, habit gives rise to a new
intensity, and for the first time the piece begins to feel familiar to
me. I sense a new mastery over my own experience. But the more

I gain in experience, the less the thing I am experiencing can be distinguished from experience itself. This means that, as I listen and re-listen to this piece, the uniqueness of my role as a listener is soon reduced to being an extended critique of every single time that I have listened to this music, all the way up to the present moment. It's as though my first experience with the music has been elevated exponentially by my re-listening. For the first time, I try out my ability to return and relate to my first listening, and then again, also for the first time, I try to relate that re-listening to the next, and so on and so forth.

What we are talking about is just a dulling sensation, not the feeling of total disappearance. As long as we are alive, we are constantly running into sensations, impressions, and ideas for the first time. But the way that we understand the feeling of the first time also grows dimmer, and we increasingly interpret any new first time as if it were just another instance of all the other things that we have done in our lives. While growing up and ageing, a living organism endowed with a memory gets better at recognising for the first time what doing something for the first time does to all the subsequent times that we do something. In this way, 'the first time' loses its immediacy and instead turns into a kind of exponent, a power equal to n experiences in the past. Living an absolutely intense life turns out to be a paradoxical affair; the fervent followers of 'the first time' believe it to be the supreme intensity; according to their calculations, the most we can ever hope for is to raise an experience to the power of one. For them, there can be no greater exponent than pure singularity.

The memory of a culture or a civilisation fills out as life passes and time marches on. And the more this happens, the more our experiences of doing something for the first time become meta-experiences. We might even say that postmodernity, as theorised at the end of the twentieth century, was modern culture's experience of being conscious of its own modernity for the first time. At the end of the day, postmodernity turns out to be yet another ruse meant to counteract the routine of modernity. Nothing modern could be felt directly any longer and, for the first time, the 'postmodern' mind experienced the impossibility of feeling anything (a strain of music, the plot of a novel, a scene in a film, or a political idea) for the first time. There were no longer any firsts; now every first time would always begin as a second time. There is always something intensely innocent about the first time that we arrive at the end of innocence. Then another innocence comes to light, but this time it's a little less intense and little bit stale. We realise that even the end of innocence no longer astonishes us; we already know all too well what that loss is like. Subjected to the merciless effects of routine, the intensity of the first time becomes increasingly dull, albeit without ever being totally annihilated. And now it seems that we are out of options. All resistance against the ultimate mechanisation of our thinking is futile.

Life's only hope is the opposite of life

As was done in modernity, we can always commit ourselves to sustaining intensities, and join the endless war against the destruction wrought by habit. But now we have an understanding of the relentless logic that causes people to collapse when they are subjected to the norm of intensity. As time passes, the *more* of feeling always ends up being *less*.

This routine is the sentimental clockwork that explains our exhaustion, discouragement, and ethical downfalls. These effects of routine have nothing to do with reason itself; instead they follow a kind of rationality of perception, one that paradoxically allows us to perceive the intensities of life at the same time that it works against them. We can come up with infinite ways of renewing perception. Unfortunately, routine still wins out in the end. No matter what we do, something within our perception eventually catches on to the regularity of things, and we figure out that the absence of rules is just a rule like any other. All of our efforts to vary, to increase intensities, and to preserve the force of the unprecedented are of little use. When we rely exclusively on intensity to find a reason for living, we end up surrendering both life and thought to the fatigue of existence. Modernity accidentally shook an invincible monster from its slumber, and now we find it here, half hidden within the depths of our feelings.

When it comes to remembering a sensation, the effect of routine is superior to all conceivable intensifications. This monster has nothing to do with our understanding of the situation. Routine feeds off everything that appears and reappears; anyone who would claim to fight routine through the fanatical intensification of their existence must still not understand that in the end they strengthen routine all the more by fostering an even greater routine of intensities. The intelligent person who believes in beating routine through creation and novelty makes this mistake: she provokes the growth of the very exhaustion that she struggles to overcome. Creation and novelty themselves soon become tiresome.

Albeit out of self-defence, this is exactly what the once intense but now intensive person triggered in modern culture, a routine of intensities that permeates most of the areas of our existence. And the consequences are disastrous for our ethical situation. By giving ourselves over to intensity and making it the guiding star of our lives, our desire for new intensities has no other choice but to chase after the *absence of intensity*. Whoever surrenders without reservation to the raging forces of life finishes up cornered by routine and unable to hope for anything stronger than the disappearance of those forces. Although it was once thought to be absolute, and by the same token without opposite, the truth is that intensity cannot help but produce its own opposite. This is why representations of a final deliverance from all intensities regularly surface in human cultures, specifically in the forms of wisdom and salvation. Why does this happen? Life is so versatile that, over the course of a sufficiently lengthy existence, it begins to wear on itself. The feeling of life within us tires of its own demands and starts to wonder about the negation of life. Every life that is even the slightest bit conscious and that relies only on living and on its fundamental intensity will sooner or later desire to affirm its opposite. The opposite of such a life is not death, but rather an existence beyond the prison of variable intensities and the prospect of endless progress.

What we have called 'electric modernity' is on its last legs and can no longer tell us how or why we continue to exist. But beyond it, we see the reappearing philosophical and religious promises that had long been eclipsed by the idea of intensity. Taking advantage of the routine that lurks behind the enthusiasm promised by the modern age, our exhausted consciousness begins to feel the temptation of wisdom and religious salvation once more.

Notes

1. In *Form and Object* 'chance' and 'price to pay' operate very much like, respectively, 'transcendence' and 'facticity' for Sartre. The former denotes contingency and genuine opportunity, usually for Garcia the result of some form of constitutive underdetermination or aporia. But when one takes advantage of a chance, other opportunities are foreclosed and characteristic, albeit often unforeseen, consequences follow. This is the price. As exemplified above in his dialectic of routine, Garcia's heavy stress on the price one must always pay is what makes him fundamentally a tragic thinker.

2. In Marcel Proust's *Swann's Way*, Charles Swann hears the same piece of music, the fictional Vinteuil Sonata, which he refers to as the 'little phrase by Vinteuil'. Proust, *Swann's Way*, p. 305. However, it seems different to Swann every time he hears it. Garcia's *petite phrase* seems to refer to Swann's *petite phrase*, which varies through repetition.

3. In music, *prima volta* designates that a passage is to be played through the first time but omitted in the repetition.

7

An Opposing Idea

Trapped in the Ethical Vice

Life makes things intense, thought makes things equal[1]

The representation of a non-intense state of life shelters every consciousness from the exhaustion of perceptions, experiences, and ideals. Our last hope requires us to use thought to imagine a completely equal state of life, one without highs and lows, a world where there is no such thing as too little or too much. The last refuges of the spirit threaten to disappear when an individual or a community starts to feel the fatal weakening of the intensity of everything they believe, know, and experience. Things once held to be beautiful, true, and good are still beautiful, true, and good. Yet something about them has become less exciting. In such cases, only one thing allows for the spirit to hold out hope of finding sanctuary.

We can provisionally define *thought* as a part of certain living organisms that is not structured around intensities; thought begins from the premise that all things are *equal*. Thought is the unfeeling part at the heart of a being with feelings. Thought is the part that does not suffer in a suffering being. Living things are traversed by all sorts of variable intensities, but thought refers to that part of living things that is instead dedicated to the search for things that never vary and stay identical. There is no reason to believe that thought, in this sense of the word, is particular to something in living things that is superior, more elevated, or more noble. Defining thought as the search for the equality of things instead of as a search for intensity need not imply any value judgement. Nor is it necessary to act as if thought were the exclusive province of the human species. On the contrary, there's a kind of thought in all perceiving things. This sort of thought sets into motion the part of all animal perception that identifies, classifies, recognises, quantifies, and calculates. This part of the animal is based around identities; it goes to work on intensities by cutting the world up into pieces and categorising everything. From the very outset, thinking something entails a loss of the ability to tell whether that thing is more or less what it is. Thinking makes everything equal in precisely this sense: after passing through the realm of thought, nothing is lessened, reduced, or destroyed. That which I conceive as possible exists no less, in my thought, than that which I conceive as real. The more or less real character of an entity only becomes visible outside the medium of thought. In the realm of thought, all things exist at the same level.

Consider the following example: I think and imagine a tree with golden fruit. Now, the object that I imagine is not real. Limited to the present state of botany, the only way to experience the apples that I imagine with my own eyes would be to go to an orchard, find the nearest apple tree, and give it a light dusting with a can of gold spray paint. Can thought alone allow me to show that this tree with golden fruit doesn't really exist? Kant declared that existence is not a real predicate, and from at least that moment on it has been generally agreed that the resources of thought are insufficient to distinguish between what is or is not real.[2] Thought has to be backed up by experience and sensory perception; thought must be supported by the eyes, the ears, and the nerves. Inasmuch as they are both thought, something that exists in the imagination exists neither more nor less than something that really exists. Thought equalises the ontological status of all things.

Is it ever possible for thought alone to judge whether one kind of object exists more or less than any other? In many schools of philosophy, contradictory objects are often treated as if they somehow exist less than other kinds of objects. Such objects are held to be nonexistent because they correspond to two contradictory concepts that are impossible to unify. Because they are pure objects of thought, a squared circle or a tree that isn't a tree seem to exist *a little less* than a circle or a tree. Nonetheless, as long as a contradictory object is conceivable in the most minimal way, the very fact that it is somehow also a determinate object means that one contradictory object can never be exactly the same as any other. Even if the old logical principle (*ex contradictione sequitur quodlibet*) holds true, and anything can follow from a contradiction, one contradiction is still never the same as any other contradiction.[3] A squared circle is not the same as a triangular circle. The difference between them may be a weak one, but it is a difference all the same. Likewise, for thought, a contradictory object is neither more nor less something than the tree I see in front of me. As far as thought is concerned, being something only means being *neither more nor less*. 'Something' refers to that which remains impervious to the variable ontological intensities. Everything that is something is *equally* something.

Objects of thought have equal ontological dignity. Nothing that has ever been conceived exists more strongly or more weakly than anything else that has ever been thought. This makes it possible to identify thought as the operation through which a living organism distinguishes between all things, the good and the bad, the beautiful and the ugly, and the existent and the nonexistent. Maybe this is why absoluteness, eternity, perfection, and simplicity are the guiding values of pure thought in numerous cultures. Having been completely abstracted from perception, thought tends to isolate its objects; it unifies objects and wrests them from the ravages of time. Thought gives us a world where the values of sentient life such as variation, development, and, more generally, intensity, are flipped on their heads.

Left to its own devices, thought is oblivious to intensity. Everything we think of gets *identified* as soon as we think it.

Now we can understand why the very same part of thought that gets introduced into every perception in order to sustain a real intensity also ends up neutralising that intensity in one fell swoop. What we have called the 'effect of routine' is actually born out of the indistinct blending of thought and life, and the melange of equalisation and intensification that affect all animal perception.

Now it should be possible to see how the exhilarating image of electricity trained modern consciousness to think of models for life and to usurp in the name of thought the intense character once supposed to lie at the heart of life itself. Having become intensive little by little, the intense person hoped to impose life on thought and tried to introduce shock, explosiveness, variation, and modulations of electrified sensation into their conception of the world. The way that we categorised our knowledge was based on ideas of development and processuality, not fixity and substantiality. Those categories were made to serve our vital interests, and made it seem as if we have to think in the same way that we live. Living and thinking both had to be done intensely.

And yet by introducing the values of life into thought, we forget how thought affects life. Thought nullifies life. Thought causes this nullification because it always treats its objects as if they were identities. Just as we have been arguing throughout this inquiry, here again we see that identification works against intensification.

By striving to make the values of life into absolute values, a living being can stoke the flames of life and heighten their intensity until we seem to catch a glimpse of the incandescence of the ideal itself. Nevertheless, inasmuch as that living being is also a thinking being, all of this activity proves counterproductive, and can only conclude in the de-intensification of what it had meant to intensify all along. The ravages of individual and collective exhaustion, and the resulting immense fatigue that began to afflict modern culture, all eventually force the *life* within us to desire something that *thought* indicates is *less intense*. Left to itself, human thought breathes life into traditional ways of representing the nullification of the intense. It maps out a world that fits with the classical values of identity, simplicity, eternity, and the absolute. Thought begins to daydream of a world of spectral states of the self that are totally free of all intensity. It also dreams up the image of a residue left behind after the body has finally been liberated and purified of its organic variations. We commonly call this residue the soul or the spirit. This process is aimed at filtering out affects (the passions), and leads to two fundamental operations of human thought: the quest for wisdom and the pursuit of salvation.

When all of life's intensities burn out, the life within us is drawn to thought's lack of intensity. When we ask just what that might be, we are presented with a phantasmatic image of how our being will remain absolutely, simply, and eternally the best of what it is. This is the image of a body that has finally stopped being subjected to the *more* or *less* of perception, a body free from all the impulses that course through it and make organic existence what it is. Thought allows us to imagine a similar kind of liberation in terms of either transfiguration or nullification. It all comes down to a choice between salvation and wisdom.

Thanks to wisdom

People shaped by the modern fascination with electricity were not looking to become wise. The libertine, the romantic, and the electrified adolescent all saw traditional wisdom as a kind of renunciation. First the intense person scoffed at the mastery and domestication of the body by the spirit; then the intensive person found such disciplines to be equally laughable. In the eyes of these new kinds of people, wisdom was a cowardly means of trying to escape from life by levelling out all of its exhilarating ups and downs. Being wise is effectively a kind of equanimity that allows us to avoid the lofty peaks and deep valleys of our own moods and passions. In this sense, being wise means working towards a systematic de-intensification of the self.

There are numerous examples of such wisdom. In Buddhism, the cycle of rebirth is represented by endlessly variable processes. We imagine that the intensity of the world is like a stream, a great river flowing on without end, and we think of the passage of souls from body to body called universal transmigration. Captives of suffering, all souls are held prisoner by the very fact that impermanence is a part of the very nature of feeling. What is *saṃsāra* if not a tremendous, fascinating image of the flowing movement of all beings? We've already seen how electric current replaced the current of a flowing river in the modern imaginary, and took its place as a new symbol of becoming and perpetual change. When we think of *saṃsāra*, we imagine a state in which all intensities are really one. What we picture is a kind of universal intensity. After his vision of *saṃsāra*, Siddhārta Gautama's whole aim is to find a way to liberate the souls that would otherwise be condemned to suffer at the hands of this universal cycle of oscillations. Practice, meditation, and prayer became means of trying to neutralise this intensity. In this way, the wisdom of the Buddha relies upon the promise that, little by little, self-discipline can make it possible to nullify the intensities that hold every being in their thrall.

But this nullification is not specific to Buddhism. The passions branch out from the body and spread into thought, so the sage's task generally consists of using the mind's ability to stabilise and even out the mood. This stability is gradually transmitted to the nerves, muscles, heart, and stomach. The Stoics' rigorous preparations for *ataraxia*, a state wherein the soul is no longer troubled by the passions, are also bound up with this effort to attenuate the impact of the excessive drives of life on our minds. The intensities of life make the equal part of our soul a slave to the variable, ephemeral part of us. Therefore, the goal is to make the former independent of the latter.

Most human societies have made such promises of wisdom. There are any number of disciplines that try to carry out a slow, painstaking process of spiritual undermining in order to attenuate and weaken all of the intensive values of life.

The following are examples of some classical ways of picturing wisdom: the withdrawal of the senses (*pratyahara*), the yogic identification of *ātman* with *brahman* (the self and the whole), the ideal of a smooth surface that reflects the world without disturbing it, and the notion of pure flatness found in some of the schools of Zen Buddhism. The same thing is also at work in the kinds of concentration, introspection, and visualisation designed to neutralise internal and external disturbances. These can be found in Vedic religion, Sufi meditation, Jainism, and Stoicism. Every wisdom seems to have initially focused on decreasing the variation of the intensities of a living subject. They aimed to level the sine wave of life into an even plane by sucking anything that perceives, desires, remembers, suffers, or enjoys out of the spirit. Western philosophy preserved the ethical part of this project of making a human subject possessed of both equanimity and *equality*. Needless to say, such a subject is also devoid of intensity. Here, as in Descartes' *Passions of the Soul*, the point is to simultaneously 'equalise the passions' and make ourselves seem at one with the world by progressively renouncing the tension that pits our desires against our needs.

As we have defined it here, wisdom is an operation that most human thought has in common. Wisdom acts directly on the intensities of life. Rather than trying to go beyond them, wisdom instead tries to progressively reduce them to zero. To this end, wisdom promises that consciousness will be able to access a peaceful state in which variation is no longer of interest and can no longer agitate the soul.

Now we can see how the electric ideal made modernity into an especially peculiar moment in the moral history of humanity. Modernity was the attempt to present humanity with an ethical goal other than wisdom; in many respects, that goal was even opposed to wisdom. Wisdom traditionally understood the purpose of life in terms of the nullification of life. Modern life instead pinned its hopes on an endless increase of the intensity of all things.

Thanks to salvation

To a modern mind forced to reckon with intensities, it looked as though wisdom promised a kind of end through *nullification*. But unlike wisdom, salvation tries to go beyond the variable intensities of life by instead imagining a kind of *transfiguration*, and hoping for a supreme, sovereign state of existence in which intensities will never again vary. But the intensities of life are maximised, not minimised, when the blessed enter God's kingdom to receive their eternal reward.[4] Indeed, the intensities of life become maximised to the highest level possible, a point where everything becomes so strong that afterwards nothing can be *more* or *less* any more.

The religious promise of salvation rests on the possibility of preserving the self after it has been purified of the variable intensities of emotion, from sadness and joy, to love and hate. The self is then supposed to be transfigured; it loses its intensive self-identity and is changed into a simple form of identity that is both perfect and absolute. After being saved, I identify with my soul, the pure and permanent part of my being. Wisdom tries to reduce the intensity of the self to zero, but salvation envisions an intensity of the self so powerful that nothing could ever be more powerful. The self will be saved; it will exist definitively and enjoy its true life, whether it be in Paradise or in the bosom of God. Being saved ensures that the intensity of the self, that variable and wandering identity that always changes as long as I live, will be exalted to the point of being absolute. Faith promises salvation by way of a qualitative change that makes the greatest of all intensities stop being an intensity at all. What does it mean to be saved? It means definitively being what is the truest in me. It means being what I am completely, purely, simply, and for all eternity. It is to be forever seated at the hand of the Saviour, who is, for believers, God, the lord and creator of the world.

That is the promise of Islam and Christianity. More broadly, what is now offered to anxious people is the same as the great hope of humanity before the advent of modernity and electricity. It is the hope that there is an end to the intensities of life and the anxiety of being.

We must of course point out the difference between two different types of salvation that often become muddled together in French, but which are clearly distinguished in some other languages. In German, for example, there are the words *Erlösung*, which refers to a kind of negative liberation, a release *from*, and the word *Heil*, which instead refers to a kind of positive replenishment. All salvation is *de facto* the promise of a way out of intensities. It promises that there will be no more of the ups and downs of pleasure and pain. It offers an end to *more* and *less*, and an escape from the cycle of repeated existence in different bodies. Salvation is instead the prospect of the absolute, a maximal intensity of life that is both the last and only one. Faith in salvation is the belief in a maximal and final intensity. For thought, salvation means the possibility of experiencing a force of life so powerful that it takes us outside of life itself. It signals the path beyond, to a state that is radically incommensurable with organic life. Humanity struggles to imagine what such a state might be like; our understanding of it is always far from perfect.

In Islam and Christianity, salvation is at once an image and an idea; it is the image and idea of a liberation from sin, suffering, and the deceptions of life, because a life spent searching after intensity here below can never merit the glory of the absolute life there above. Nevertheless, thought can wing its way close to those heavenly heights. This means that the incorruptible part of the living organism – thought's own idealisation of itself, the spirit – can be communicated to the body, just as the body manages to communicate the action of the passions to the mind. Paradise is still the most popular image for the liberation that culminates in a maximal intensity and defies all representation. It's said that in Paradise, humanity will want for nothing, and there will be no more hunger, fear, or doubt. Paradise is depicted in the Qur'an as something more like a maximal intensity of life. It is an absolutely sweet, luxurious existence, where no pleasure ever comes up short, and where all believers are now one family. Adorned with silk and gold, the blessed eat and drink the finest delicacies and satisfy their sexual needs without frustration. In the biblical representation of Heaven, the emphasis is instead placed on being delivered from the variable intensities of life. Rather than being promised the maximally intense satisfaction of their spiritual and carnal desires, believers are instead assured that they will be liberated from the shackles of desire itself.

Wisdom and salvation share certain symmetries. They might seem to be opposed to one another, but we can also see wisdom and salvation as two horizons, two different ways that might make it possible to wrench ourselves free from the great carousel of the variable intensities of life and escape the circus of it all. Wisdom and salvation entered into all of the promises of philosophy and religion, albeit to varying degrees. And this continued to be the case right up until an electric ethics came along and gave modern people the idea that life could have a new and different kind of meaning.

A Dilemma

Wisdom and salvation both managed to mobilise the intensity of life, the enthusiasm of the heart, and the notion of the exaltation of the whole of a being. Nevertheless, wisdom and the promises of salvation end up imposing models from our thinking on to the values of our lives. The very principle of thought, its equal character, begins to prevail over the intense character that is the very principle of sentient life. Among all the philosophical purveyors of wisdom, just as in all the religions that instill a hope for salvation in humanity, thought's ability to imagine an equal state of existence triumphs over the variable intensities that are transmitted to us by sensation. Wisdom and salvation both stand as a sign of the imposition of thought upon the living.

Electric ethics, however, gave life victory over thought. We have already traced how that ethics emerges and ends up giving shape to our modern style of humanity. In countless ways, this ethics ordered us to bring what we think into line with what we feel as living beings. This meant that now our knowledge, practices, desires, hopes, morality, and politics would all be structured around one cardinal value, intensity. Or, to be more precise, we can at least say that this reorientation happened for that part of our humanity that was trying to make progress and blaze a trail beyond the ruts made by premodern ways of life.

First, the promise of intensity gave shape to a new form of ethics, one faithful to the force of life. That promise managed to eclipse the old promises of being able to nullify or transfigure life through thought. However, after being subjected to the effects of routine, the promise of intensity was fatally exhausted. Intensity was forced to again make way for the old ideas of wisdom and salvation. This is why, to the modern mind, it seems as if wisdom and religion are making a comeback. But the truth is that they were here all along. Put simply, today it looks as if the fascination with electricity is no longer strong enough to sustain the individual and collective promise of a life for which the best we can hope is its intensification. Now we can see that it is impossible to perpetually maintain intensities, since to strengthen them is also to weaken them. This means that the promise of intensity is not enough to satisfy the ethical needs of our humanity. As soon as the popular notion of intensity was elevated to a position where it began to preside over life, each and every one of us felt as if we were left with nothing but the prospect of an ineluctable, almost mechanical, future exhaustion. Every individual or collective organism that unreservedly gives itself over to intensity in this way is dragged into a vague depression, a slow sinking of excitement, and a fatal nullification that can only end by collapsing.

The thousands of detours taken in each of our singular existences end up leading us to a contradiction that we confront: wanting to increase our life does nothing other than decrease it.

This is the first horn of the dilemma. By pursuing the modern ethical project, we condemn ourselves to reducing thought to the intense feeling of life in a way that weakens thought to almost nothing. The second horn entails turning our backs on this modernity and relying on the same hope already yearned for by so many people before us. It means striving after a state of equality, one as pure and perfect as thought itself. The sage and the cleric believe that thought allows them to reach certain truths, and they try to live their lives according to those truths. Fascinated by the nature of electricity and interpreting every-thing in terms of intensity, both modern humanity and then contemporary humanity[5] instead tried to align their truths, ideas, and beliefs with the intense qualities of their bodies. And there you have it: the horns of this dilemma catch us once more; no matter how we approach it, we always finish up losing. We can either ruin our feeling of intensity a little more for the sake of defending it, or we can go on the attack against intensity and again pin our hopes on wisdom, salvation, and a way out of this life.

The intensity of life gets lost in both cases. But we have to choose, and we have to determine which approach is more just, ethically speaking. If ethics is more about *ways* of doing things, and less about what particular thing is done, then the point of ethics is to determine or invent a manner of life that would be faithful to the feeling of living. In other words, ethics must find a way to keep from weakening our feeling of being alive. A *moral* life is a life led according to certain moral ideals. It's a determined life. Regardless of which moral or political ideals end up determining it, an *ethical* life is a life that neither reduces nor nullifies a living person's feeling of being alive. From this point of view, ethics always returns, gen-eration after generation, to referee the dispute between thought's colonisation of our lives, and life's colonisation of our thought. And it is at precisely this point that we arrive at an ethical decision that seems to be impossible for us to make.

Dead end

Our ethical condition can be summed up in a few words; we are now caught in a deadlock between two opposing ethical pos-sibilities that ultimately end up being the same. One option is to hold on to the modern promises surrounding the intensification of life and thought and to give up the slightest hope of finality or transcendence. The other option is to surrender to the promises that existed well before modernity, promises that the intensities of life will be nullified or transfigured as we move towards a final, transcendent horizon. Say we split up into two groups. On one side are those of us who decide to remain faithful to the electric promise that modern reason will endlessly intensify our lives. On the other side are those who prefer to line up behind the promises of wisdom or salvation. Either we let our lives be guided by the hope that thought can be subjected to the values of life, or we let our lives be guided by the hope that life can be subjected to the values of thought.

The choice is indeed a tragic one. It is necessary to choose, but it's impossible to do so without losing the very meaning of intensity in the process. As we have seen, leading a life with the sole purpose of intensifying it makes us susceptible to the effects of routine. Little by little, it nullifies the intensities of life in the name of those very same intensities. It is also what got us stuck in the ethical deadlock of modernity. However, trying to do the opposite with the purpose of neutralising or transfiguring the intensity of life means equating the maximum intensity possible with the disappearance of intensity. It means always hoping for a state of *ataraxia*, or apathy, or grace, or deliverance, all of which signal the return to a premodern ethics. Nothing is a priori forbidden. Maybe we have to go back and hope for wisdom or salvation in order to rediscover the meaning of an intense life. But the promises of wisdom or salvation are no more faithful than intensive modernity was to the intensity of the feeling of life. They use the intensity of the feeling of life as a means of negating that same feeling. Wisdom and salvation have to call upon the enthusiasm of people who live, feel, and suffer in order to promise an end to suffering, a transmutation of feeling, and a final completion of life. The whole trick is to intensely believe in something other than intensity. In either case, intensity doesn't hold up. Whether voluntarily or involuntarily, intensity is destined to disappear because it isn't sustained by the mind. Does this mean that we have to live with the sole mission of making our lives more intense? If so – alas! – we have just condemned ourselves to be less and less capable of doing so. Should we instead live with the aim of suppressing the intensities of life? We cannot decide to do that without already making use of the intensity of life and our nervous enthusiasm. Doing so means betraying intensity by turning it against itself.

In both cases, what is lost is intensity itself, our feeling of feeling.

No matter which choice we make, it seems that we still have no sustainable way of using thought to preserve this intensity of life. Whether you attack it or defend it, the intensity of life cannot be maintained. It cannot be sustained throughout an entire existence, and it cannot support an entire society.

At this juncture, we cannot help but wonder how it might be possible to remain faithful to the intensity of life without making it the absolute principle of life or trying to nullify it wholly or in part. In short, how can we live in a way that maintains the intensity of our lives to the best of our ability? Our ethical consciousness is trapped between a rock and a hard place. On one side, we are crushed by the exhaustion of all the absolutely intense things promised to us by modernity; it is as if we are still supposed to believe that such a promise, one already past its prime, could suffice alone. On the other side, we get caught up in a resurgence of philosophical and religious promises regarding how to extinguish or sublimate the illusory life of the body. On the one hand, we sentence ourselves to the plodding, wearisome extinction of our vitality. On the other hand, we lose ourselves in the intellectual negation of the intrinsic value of life. The battle seems to be lost before it has begun. What can be done if you still believe that the goal of life is to maintain its intensity the best you can for as long as you can? Living with the sole aim of staying faithful to the force of life within oneself seems to make us helpless.

Maybe it is not possible to think and live in a way that neither subjects thought to life nor life to thought. Maybe it is futile for people to want to live *more* or *less* while trying to find a way to think, no *more*, no *less*. Maybe there is no sustainable way to live without thinking *intensely* or to think without *levelling* life out. Maybe our condition is a dead end.

Notes

1. It is important to reiterate that the manner in which thought necessarily interprets the world in this chapter gives rise to the world
   of *Form and Object*'s Book I. Such a world is a flat, non-intensive
   one. In this kind of world, no entity is more or less itself than any
   other entity. In *Form and Object*, Garcia argues that our philosophical accounts must presuppose such a flat world, and in the current
   work he presents it as phenomenologically necessary. Nevertheless,
   Garcia here neither alludes to nor references some of his most striking theses about *Form and Object*'s extensive world, such as: 1) the
   manner in which entities of necessity frustrate reductionism; 2) how
   these entities bifurcate into two modes, that of object and that of
   thing; 3) the manner in which this bifurcation allows one to avoid
   both metaphysical holism and atomism; 4) the divorce of unity and
   being; 5) the consequent sense in which numerosity and identity
   are holistically determined for Garcia; and 6) the inconsistent nature
   of this world's limits. Regarding the latter thesis, Garcia holds that
   at the top this world is inconsistent with itself, while at the bottom
   the world is inconsistent with the matter that composes it. For an
   explication of these properties, see Chapters 1 to 7 of Cogburn's
   Garcian Meditations. As noted in the Translators' Introduction, for an
   analogue in analytic philosophy to Garcia's claims about the necessary connections between thought and feeling, one could do no
   better than John McDowell's reflections on these themes, starting
   with his canonical *Mind and World*. Much of McDowell's work is an
   extended meditation on the Kantian claim to the effect that there
   are no perceptions without thought. Finally, for an interpretation
   of vagueness very much of a piece with Garcia's insistence that
   thought constitutively treats entities as if they were identities, an
   account that turns standard analytic accounts since Russell on their
   head, see Jon Cogburn and Franklin Worrell's 'S-Vagueness and
   R-Vagueness, Some Results from Counterexamples to the Underlying Comparative Theory'.
2. This is from Kant's discussion in the *Critique of Pure Reason* of the
   ontological proof for the existence of God. The ontological proof
   concludes that God must exist from the fact that a perfect being that
   did not exist would not be perfect. This follows from the claim that
   it is better to exist than not to exist. Kant argues that affirming such
   premises involves predicating existence on a thing. But, according
   to Kant, existence is not a predicate. Rather, we predicate properties

of things that already exist. Garcia's claim about how philosophers generally responded to this by taking thought to be insufficient to determine existence is plausible, at least for a robust class of armchair metaphysicians and their critics. For armchair metaphysicians such as David Chalmers, thought is sufficient to determine what is conceptual and hence what is possible. But perception and scientific reasoning together are needed to determine which possible entities are actual. See Tamar Gendler and John Hawthorne's anthology *Conceivability and Possibility* for discussions about this debate, including a canonical statement by Chalmers.

3. Garcia originally makes this argument in *Form and Object*'s Book I, Part I, Section I where it is a part of his larger criticism of various attempts from the history of thought that denigrate the being of some classes of entities. Remember that ontological flatness involves the denial of invidious distinctions that both elevate (in a manner akin to phenomenology's elevation of human experience) and denigrate (as in the approach to the mind forwarded by eliminative reductionists) classes of entities. Contradictory entities are probably the most widely reviled in the history of philosophy. Cogburn's *Garcian Meditations* establishes connections between Garcia's work and that of Graham Priest, the most significant analytic philosopher to defend the ontological dignity of contradictory entities. For Priest, see especially *Beyond the Limits of Thought*.

4. From *Form and Object*'s Coda: 'There is no salvation, because if it were real, then it does not concern me any more, and if it concerns me, then it is not real: it absorbs me as part of a whole' (Garcia, *Form and Object*, p. 433). The discussion above might be read as an explanation of why this is true.

5. On the distinction between modern and contemporary, see *Form and Object*, Book II, Chapter VIII, 'Arts and Rules', in particular, Section 5, 'The Formation of New Arts and the Systematic Deregulation of the Ancient Arts: Classicists, Moderns, and Contemporaries'. There is a rich interplay between Garcia's genealogies of intensity in this book and his account of beauty in *Form and Object*. Of course, this is all interestingly complicated by the fact that *Form and Object*'s treatment of beauty constitutively involves intensity. For Garcia, something is beautiful to the extent that it is more intensely itself. See Chapter 9 of Cogburn's *Garcian Meditations* for a discussion of Garcia's accounts of truth, beauty, and goodness.

8

An Opposing Image

Something Resists

The eve of Seoul

There have long been stories about robots that have a human form and are capable of learning to feel emotions and to love. The word 'robot' first appeared in 1928, in Karel Čapek's play entitled *R.U.R.*, which stands for 'Rossum's Universal Robots'. The term refers to artificial beings; in this work they are presented as 'biological machines' produced on a far-flung island. At first these robots are incapable of feeling. Nevertheless, the continuing development of technology and the political demands made by their human defenders (Helena Glory's Humanity League) make it possible for the robots to gain a heart and a brain, and two of the robots even fall in love. The fantasy of a 'loving machine' recurs throughout modern times and has often served to illustrate the exhaustion of our own intensities of life. This fantasy regularly appears in the best of Osamu Tezuka's manga. The loving machine is one of the themes in Philip K. Dick's novel *Do Androids Dream of Electric Sheep?*, and this is even more the case in its cinematographic adaptation, *Blade Runner*. This obsession with sentimental machines also shows up on television in the love stories between cylons on *Battlestar Galactica* and the amorous interactions of the hubots on *Real Humans*.

At the end of *R.U.R.*, the last man finds out that the feeling of life has found its way into robotic creatures. Two robots named Primus and Helena are threatened with dissection by the architect Alquist, and each begs him to spare the life of the other. Alquist realises that they sincerely love one another and that the pair now embody the new Adam and Eve in a post-human world. In this way, the robots reinvent the life that humanity has exhausted, 'I feel so strange, I don't know what it is with me, it's silly, as if I were headless, my body aches, and my heart, everything's hurting ... I can't even tell you what's happened to me!'[1] declaims Helena, like a machine programmed for tragedy. The mouth of the robot pronounces words of anguish and passion. From then on, the vocabulary of vital intensity belongs to non-living, mechanical beings that have been awakened to that power of life that we have left lying dormant within ourselves.

Borrowing from the golem of folklore and the novel *Frankenstein*, Čapek's prophetic play presents robots as beings created by humanity. Like a god who has lived too long and is now mostly numb to life, a tired humanity bequeaths the task of reviving and maintaining life to its symbolic son.[2] Karel Čapek's brother Josef was the inspiration behind the name 'robot'. Karel wanted to replace old terms such as 'automaton' and 'android'. He first considered using the neologism *labori*, after the Latin root for 'labour', but thought that the sound of the word was lacking in elegance. He then accepted his brother's proposal to play on the Czech word *robota*, which means forced labour or drudgery. At the beck and call of their masters, Čapek's robots are soulless slaves in a modern world; however, they are made up of *organic* matter. It would still take a few years for us to imagine and start constructing robots that run on electrical energy. These kinds of electric robots are the ones that fascinate us today.

Who knows? Maybe robotics expos are today's equivalent to the salons of the early seventeenth century and their experiments with electricity.

The robot or android EveR was publicly unveiled for the first time at a 2003 event in Seoul's Kyoyuk Munhwa Hoekwan Hotel. The very name of the robot evokes both the first woman in the Bible and the notion of eternity (forever). Competing alongside a Japanese 'actroid', the EveR prototype was one of the first electronic robot-women capable of imitating human facial expressions and appearing to be happy, sad, joyful, or angry, all the while moving its head, torso, arms, and legs. The Ministry of Commerce, Industry, and Energy invited men, women, and around sixty children to watch this first public exhibition. They reacted with a combination of surprise, excitement, fear, and delight so strong that it cannot help but remind us of the stunned reactions of the bourgeois audience that witnessed Bose's experiment with the *Venus electrificata* some three centuries previously. We might say that the robotic Eve ends this chapter in the history of the excitement that the electric Venus had generated within us, and that it does so by inverting the principle underlying the Venus itself. Our encounter with the electric Venus revealed the electricity within the human creature. And now, faced with the robotic Eve, we discover humanity in the electric creature. In this way, our desires end up swapping places; instead of wanting to make humanity electric, what now fascinates us is the possibility of making electricity human. After observing EveR's soft silicone face – which was modelled using a synthesis of the faces of two Korean actresses – and the movement of EveR's lips and eyes from left to right and right to left, it is easy to see how people would fall in love with an electric machine that can mimic sensations and emotions. And we suddenly find ourselves right back in the shocking embrace of the *Venus electrificata*. We don't really know why, but we are both attracted and repulsed by the life of inorganic things and the irrepressible desire for artificial being.

EveR's still-hesitant movements, its limited range of expressions, and the awkwardness of its reactions move us because they let us catch a glimpse of a purer, less intensive life. What is sighted in that moment is a sort of childhood for a humanity that has grown tired of itself. Now we hope to find again in the electronic creature the same soul that we fear we have worn out through use.

EveR is actually more of an *electronic* creature than an *electric* one. When we see it, we don't think of electricity. We think of the information that electricity broadcasts and transmits. The robot is still ahead of its time, the creature of an *age to come*. In the electronic age, data is transmitted by electric current, but electricity no longer excites our imagination; now it is little more than a commodity capable of transporting information. In fact, since the 1960s, developments in electronics have entailed the utilisation of smaller and smaller electrical charges; research has primarily focused on making advances in transmission.

Perhaps electronics are nothing other than a kind of de-intensification of electricity.

The electronic promise

If we begin to desire robots, it is simply because the life within us has become bored by the routine of its own intensity. That boredom causes the life within us to lose interest in anything that isn't mechanical. We become fascinated by things that are not really alive but appear to be living. We show our desire for the electronic way of life through our preference for synthetic music, our heightening of eroticism through the use of vibrating objects and virtual stimulation, our daily contact with touch screens and the internet of things, and through our fantasies about a technological singularity that will come to take over for an antiquated form of humanity. The more we desire the electronic way of life, the more we demonstrate the weakening of our vital desire *for* vital desire; our desire exposes the investment of our libido in things that do not live off intensity.

What is the electronic age? It is the product of the exhaustion of electricity's role as the universal agent and protagonist of technological development. The weak electrical charges that are used to transmit electronic information are related to the lack of a need for intensity in electric communication. Why spend a lot of energy on something that needs very little energy to be communicated? Intensity is now just the *means*, not the *end*. Beginning in the nineteenth century, the fantasy of remotely transmitting images combined with the photoelectric properties of selenium, thereby opening the way to using electricity as a simple tool for encoding data from light and sound. Willoughby Smith, an electrical engineer working in telegraphy, studied the characteristics of selenium. He found that, as selenium is heated, its resistance to electrical current diminishes. This made it possible to think that we could convert the effects of variations of light into an electric impulse. It would then be possible to turn light into electronic data, encode it, and transmit it over long distances. This transmission of data through light made it possible to remotely reconstitute basic data and reconstruct images that had been transmitted. One of the properties of selenium allows it to act on an electric current. The degree of its effect varies proportionately with the exposure of the element to light. In 1878, and without any prior discussion, three different researchers simultaneously proposed to use this property of selenium as a means of remotely transmitting photographic images. The Portuguese researcher Adriano de Paiva called it a 'telescope', while the French researcher Constantin Senlecq and the American George Carey instead dubbed it a 'telectroscope'.

While selenium is a distant ancestor of the 'tele-vision', it never managed to live up to people's lofty expectations that it might be the key to converting light into electricity. However, these experiments with selenium did inaugurate the age of a new fantasy, namely, that we might be able to break down both light and image into information, and then broadcast it as a signal. According to this fantasy, electricity is no longer anything but a vehicle for information. As a result, there are fewer calls for the expenditure of large amounts of energy; on the contrary, the less energy required by a thing, the more useful and economical it becomes. Our obsession thus imperceptibly shifts away from intensity and instead becomes attached to information. As though half-asleep, without even realising it, we therefore entered into a new dream that is still transforming our ethical condition. This is the electronic dream, in which the robot becomes the face of our desire.

Once the sole domain of intensity, information is now extensive. Dealing with information requires us to break down, analyse, process, calculate, and reconstruct the variations of all kinds of things, including sound, light, tactile pressure, and electricity. This is done piece by piece using quantities (expressed in shannons) of binary elements called bits. The concept of information closes the chapter opened by our electrical obsession. We are now back in the same trap from which electrical intensity was supposed to save us, quantification, the division of things *partes extra partes*, the universal calculation of everything *bit by bit*. And while spatial extension only applies to physical matter, information has a much greater breadth of application because information allows us to reduce any given to a quantity that can be compared to other quantities. These givens include all perceptible and imperceptible data, all fluctuations, and all expenditures of energy. And so information makes it possible to reduce all intensities to comparable quantities.

The spread of electronics in human technologies was a clear signal of the end of the great electric fantasy. For several decades, we have seen proof all around us that electricity is no longer anything but a humble, neutral, and discrete servant entrusted with packets, bits, and bytes of information. Since the last third of the twentieth century, nobody has been surprised by or marvelled at the power of electricity. Such an enthusiasm seems old fashioned and reminds us of the nineteenth-century imagination. That is what we find, for instance, in the steampunk trend in science fiction, in which electricity is still a source of wonder because it never became harnessed at the industrial level during the Victorian period. In our time, electrical current and its wonderful intensity have been replaced in our imagination by computers, data analysis, and the digital world. The ethics of intensity had lifted the hearts of humankind since the eighteenth century, but then it tiptoed back out of our dreams. Its influence decreased along with the decreasing role allotted to electrical current in our fantasies. The unprecedented alliance of an idea with an image allowed us to make intensity into a supreme value of life. Indeed, it seems that that is what we call modernity. The image once supplied by electrical current continued to serve a purpose even after it no longer generated the same enthusiasm. Intensity still managed to function as an ethical ideal in liberal, consumer society. But, undermined by the effects of routine, intensity lost its picturesque allure.

The electric ethics of modernity was for humanity like a vast vein of fossil fuel, and now it has been depleted. Does this mean that we have to imagine an *electronic ethics* of tomorrow? Do we have to think of a new way of being human, one inspired by our fascination with robots, just because long ago we tried to do the same and use electrical energy as a model for being human? Transhumanist thinking will give rise to an abundant variety of electronic ethics in the years to come. These will offer us the ability to go beyond our organic, sensate, electric life in favour of a life modelled on robots, artificial intelligence, and electronic creatures. That life will promise to minimise suffering, sickness, and death. We will be able to cognitively process information at a superior level, and we will gain improved mental capacities for memory, integration, and recognition, all in exchange for our vital intensities. When an image and an idea forge an alliance, we find the promise of a new ethical condition. This happened long ago with electricity and intensity, and it is happening now with electronics and information.

But all that the electronic promise can deliver is a technological version of wisdom and salvation. The electronic promise swings the pendulum back from the intensity of life, forcing itself on to thought towards the information of thought forcing itself on to life. That promise in no way extricates us from the ethical vice that traps our conscience in its clutches. It instead merely strengthens the vice's grip. So we find ourselves pulled in two different directions at once. To one side, we have the tension between the intense life and the wisdom and salvation offered up by religions; on the other side, there is the struggle between the electric life and the electronic life that is to come. At least the electronic life allows us to realise how obsolete the ideal of electric intensity that we came up in has become. We realise this even if, in many realms of social existence, we continue to obey the modern demand to live hard, fast, and intensely. Other ideals are no doubt already in the works. Some people will believe that they should use the being of information as a model and make their lives into a summary of data that can be preserved and prolonged. The qualities of this life would not be intensified, but they would be more efficient; these would include augmented memory, increased concentration, controlled moods, and the ability to keep death at bay.

Believing in this new promise would mean that we have not learned the lesson of the exhaustion of electric ethics. It would mean wanting to reduce life to thought after having hoped to reduce thought to life. It would propose a materialist analogue of the hope for wisdom and salvation. Believing in that promise once more would drag us into a simulated version of existence, one unencumbered by organic life. To do so would allow us to yet again reduce the feeling of life to something else, or let us deduce something from it, but it will not help us *maintain* that feeling.

We are not asking for a magical mantra that would show us how to live. We only want one thing, the assurance that we can think up a way for our feeling of living to resist anything that threatens to reduce it or take away from it. We have outgrown our childish expectations that some thought might reveal the meaning of life to us or teach us the rules of existence. All we ask of an ethics is that it assure us that it is possible to live a full life *without* destroying the intensity of life itself. What is the point of living forever if we lose the feeling of living in the process? Rather than the promise of an intense life or eternal life (be it spiritual or material), what we really want is just a promise that we will be able to feel alive as long as we live.

Just expressing this demand is enough to make us realise that we need look no longer for a solution to our problem; the way we have articulated our demands already makes the solution clear. We are no longer looking to *pry our way out* of the vice that holds us prisoner. What matters now is finding a way to *hang in there and resist*.

It's a draw

The whole difficulty with ethical reasoning is that there is no definitive solution for maintaining the intensity of life in a living being. To preserve the intensity of life, a thinking being has no other choice than to constantly resist life. The electricity in our nerves and muscles courses through us, strikes us, and not only makes us feel, but also makes us feel that we are feeling. Maintaining and sustaining this electricity means learning to pit it against another value. Life resists thought and its ideals. Life must resist thought because it cannot allow itself to be reduced to the demands of words, ideas, and concepts. Life also has to resist thought's attempts to categorise it in terms of equality, simplicity, absoluteness, eternity, all of which are things that are only made accessible through thought. Conversely, thought resists life because *it* cannot get mixed up with vital intensities, firing nerves, blood pressure, and hormonal fluctuations without eventually identifying and quantifying them. Over time, thought neutralises the feeling of all of those things within us. As beings that are both thinking and living, we serve as the battleground for a perpetual struggle between the variations that come from life and the identities imposed by thought. There is no referee capable of impartially settling the tug of war between what our life requires and the demands made by our thinking. We are the ones living and thinking, and that means that we are the ones who have to pass judgement on what we each regard as the values of life and thought. The process of arbitrating between life and thought is nothing other than the ethical activity of every animal subjectivity, even if it is not specifically human. In that process of arbitration, subjectivities strive to maintain the way that they feel while gathering experience and using thought as a means of schematising their sensations. We cannot deduce how we should live or how we should think without doing violence to life and to thought. An ethical being is whomever manages to straddle this line.

Two possible betrayals delineate this being's range of action: the first consists of *thinking in order to defend life*; the second is *living according to thought*. The first betrayal is the maxim of the strong being who stands above morality and reason. The second betrayal is the principle of the wise being who remains obedient to truth. These two positions are often passed off as the expression of a superior intellect or a great wisdom, while what they really indicate is just the opposite. What they instead demonstrate is an unfortunate inability to comprehend the irreducible link between the heterogeneous values of living things and thinking things. A strong, free person, one who only thinks as a means of illuminating and defending her life, is really only manipulating words and ideas to prove, albeit more or less secretly, that she is in the right. Pursuing her own best interests, she makes herself the master of anything within her that doesn't fit with her way of life. She is searching for a truth that matches with the things that she loves and hates. Her whole existence is spent trying to make our grand ideas into a vehicle for the things she finds in reality, like her hidden desires and the internal forces that drive and propel her. Such things cannot be rationally justified. They exclusively rely on her background and her way of seeing things. She hopes that the abstract world of concepts will come down on the side of her tastes and way of life. She makes universal thought into the handmaiden of her particular way of life.

The person who lives according to the tenets of her thought, and who we think of as wise, makes a different mistake that nevertheless mirrors the error of the person who defends life from thought. The wise person thinks that she can impose a universal idea on her own particular body by sheer force of will. Her glory lies in gradually reducing the intensities of her existence to abstract entities. A person who boasts that her life is coherent because she lives according to certain principles rooted in her intellect comes to resemble a weird kind of animal tamer who swells with pride after teaching a group of animals to act just like stones. On the other hand, a person who uses thought to make her particular way of life into a universal model[3] seems no more credible than a person who sculpts animals out of stone and then treats them as if they were really living beings. In reality, this is just as true for the sage and the clergyman who subordinate the intensities of the living to the truths of thought as it is for the followers of a new electronic ethics; indeed, this is also generally true for all people who think that 'morality' demands that our abstract principles and the actions we take in life must be coherent. All of these people try to derive rules for a living world where everything is intense, but they try to derive them from a world in which nothing is intense. Life never turns out the way we expect it to be, even when we try to make it that way, because everything we run into in life is only *more* or *less*. Like an ink blot spreading across a sheet of paper, or an image that moves beyond the bounds of its original tracing, our variable perceptions always end up overflowing the divisions and identities that we use to represent things in life.

However, a similar moment of disillusion also lies in store for anyone who tries to do the opposite by making the categories of thought correspond to the movements and variations of life. Thought can never simply imitate the intensities that we feel; that imitation always comes at a price. The hope of making thought into an intense thing that can feel blinds us to its ethical consequences. By taking on the form of life, thought also gives life the shape of thought. No matter what we do, a thought that is too intense always ends up rapidly neutralising intensity and transforming it into a new identity. Everything that passes through thought comes out de-intensified and equalised in one way or another. All things end up looking as if they are determined and identified after we have a concept of them. This is the case whether we are talking about my imaginary tree with the golden fruit, or the tree that I see right there in front of me, or the light that shifts and shines as it dances through its branches. Unfortunately, by trying to make our ideas and ideals into intense, electric, and living things, modernity finished up by identifying *intensity itself*. Albeit with the best of intentions, modernity turned intensity into a concept, an object of pure thought, and stripped it of its savage irreducibility. The more that we use words and ideas to affirm the superior value of things that cannot be contained by words and ideas, the more we make this life into an abstract thing and transform its intensity into a neutral idea. We can only preserve life by using thought to distinguish life from thought itself. We have to conceptualise the difference between things that are subordinated to difference, variation, and being *more* or *less*, and other things that resist that subordination. Albeit inadvertently, any attempt to ground thinking in difference, variation, and intensity harms those values; it hastens their loss by subjecting them to the routine of feeling.

Living makes us intense, but thought makes us equal. Every thinking being must distinguish within itself between the thing that thinks and the thing that feels. These rough conceptual distinctions produce an ethical tension which is broken by believing that living a certain way entails thinking a certain way or that thinking a certain way entails living a certain way.

From thought's point of view, from life's point of view

It is clearly only from thought's point of view that life and thought can be distinguished as if they each corresponded to two entirely different concepts. From life's point of view, thought is nothing more than an intensity particular to living things. Seen from this perspective, the part of us that thinks is never completely separated from the part of us that lives, feels, and suffers.

As soon as I start thinking, it is impossible for me not to differentiate the world of things happening within me from the world of thought. The former is made up of my nervous system, which allows signals to pass from my nervous centres and be received by my brain, where they are processed and integrated. The latter is a world of simple entities; they can all be identified and re-identified, and they all exist equally. I can try to treat what I think as though it were a variable intensity, but trying to use concepts to imitate life is like pretending that I'm flying when I'm actually walking. This is precisely the transmutation that the metaphysics of intensity had looked to accomplish. By modelling itself after life, thought actually contaminates the values of life, and the intensities that I am thinking are soon neutralised and reduced to identities. The effect of routine reduces the intensity of ideas to zero. This means that thought can do nothing other than identify and differentiate. Thought chops variable intensities up into entities that are distinct but equal. From the point of view of thought, the relation between life and thought always ends up looking like a clash of civilisations.

The only way to live ethically is to think a distinction, an equal difference between the equal and the intense, between conceptualisation and sentience, between what I am inasmuch as I think and what I am inasmuch as I live. But it is precisely in living that I lose sight of this distinction. I would never be able to feel a definitive difference between what I feel and what I think. As a living, feeling being, my words and ideals will always appear as just another in the series of manifold modulations of my own sensations and life experiences.

In order to arrive at a just conception of ethics, we have to be able to imagine a double relationship between the continuous and the discontinuous: to live is to experience continuities and variable intensities; to think is to cut the world up into distinct entities. To think the difference between life and thought is to make life and thought distinct. And the contrary also holds: living the difference between life and thought means feeling the continuity and fluctuations between life and thought. Nevertheless, ethics consists of organising the life we think and the thinking we live in a way that might prevent either of them from asserting its hegemony over the other. We have to organise thought's stubborn resistance to the spontaneity of life. This spontaneity rings hollow as soon as it is expressed in words. But we also have to prevent abstract thought from imposing itself on life. We have to keep thought from telling life what it must feel and making promises that life will at last be like abstract thought after it becomes wise or finds salvation.

This is the price that a thinking being must pay for the feeling of living.

Let us imagine a ridge line high in the mountains. Our job is to walk that line without plummeting down into one side or the other of the ethical void surrounding us. Two precipices border the path of existence. On one side, there's the temptation to use life as a model for thought; this is the desire of the intense person. On the other side, there's the temptation to use thought as a model for life; this is the hope of sages and people of faith. The latter might even end up being the essence of the new electronic promise.

Ethical life is neither the life of the sage nor the life electric. It is not a quest for salvation, nor is it the spontaneous search for intensity. It is not a life given over to intensity, but it also isn't trying to escape from intensity. It is a narrow path that winds its way through all discourses. Along this path, we have no choice but to call it a draw between those who tell us to think intensely and those who order us to live equally. Giving way to either side makes one part of us a slave of the other, and we end up squandering the best part of life, its liveability. If we go one way, the liveability of life is exhausted by counterproductive affirmations; but if we go the other way, we find that that same liveability ends up being negated as we wait on the arrival of *something else*. In order neither to assert nor deny the intensity of life, we have to learn to find intensity in the experience of resistance. Only a thought that resists life can make us feel truly alive, and true thinking only happens in a life that resists thought.

Sustained by two contrary impulses, we might have a chance of walking this tightrope without losing our balance.

Chance[4]

Thinking as we have tried to here should not be about imposing theoretical conclusions on our lives. The ethical function of reasoning is not to constrain the reader, but rather to preserve the difference between things that life tends to blur and confuse. Properly conceptualised, it is finally possible for things to seem as if they are distinct yet equal, or equal yet distinct. This is the ideal of thought. Instead of trying to constrain or govern our lives, the ideal of thought attempts to present life with distinct and equal ideas that make it possible for people to live with a full knowledge of the facts.

Living is equivalent to thinking, and vice versa. But thinking well is not the same as thinking as you live, and living well is not the same as living as you think. We have to resist the temptation to make ourselves coherent. But then how are we to live? We have not laid out an ethical distinction between what we conceptualise and what we feel just so that we can ultimately subject our lives to some new law. It is not about replacing our modern, exhausted condition of being subjected to the demands of a vital intensity with some other bond of vassalage. At the end of our inquiry, we will comprehend that our goal was never to determine some moral content. We refused to let thought legislate life. It is actually quite the opposite. We no longer have to make life submit to the legislation of thought, nor do we have to make thought obey the commands of life. An ethical response to the question of how we should live consists of saying *neither* 'So that you live more intensely' *nor* 'So that you come to know truth, salvation, or the absolute.' The only truly ethical response is instead the following: 'Live in a way that doesn't make you lose the feeling of being a living organism.' Of course, as soon as we say 'we', the question changes and goes from being ethical to being political.[5] Ethics concerns itself with coming up with the best way to live, while politics determines who enters into ethical consideration. Understood in this sense, ethics can be applied to an individual just as well as a community, or to all of humanity, and maybe even to other animals besides human beings, since humans are not the only beings capable of knowing and perceiving. For us sentient beings, thought offers a point of view on life that is outside of life; life can be made to look desirable from that angle, and therein lies a possible ethical usage of our ability to think. We must not shrug off life as if it were defective or a foregone conclusion. Instead, we must make the feeling of breathing into something almost incomprehensible, and do the same for the feeling of seeing light and shadows flit and flutter as the hours tick by, and for the buzzing and humming of sounds and voices that come and go. We must renew our incomprehension of what it feels like to be a body with nerves and hormones that goes from feeling exalted, beaten down, all tired out, and finally peaceful, only to feel that we are unleashed again. We can then realise that we are not dead and that we are still changing.

Living appears almost miraculous from the point of view of the abstract world of thought. Like a curious stranger discovering an unknown land, the part of us that tends towards reflection rejoices in its ability to inhabit the world as a body. Conversely, the part of us that feels can partake in the excitement of belonging to the world as an idea.

Thus, at this inquiry's end, we come to comprehend that we can only conserve that all-important vital intensity by putting thought and life into opposition and pitting the two against each other. This means that the only conceivable ethical life requires us to obstinately refuse either to make our ideas correspond to our way of living or to force our life into the service of grand ideas. Our ethical character requires an approach that is far more delicate than all of that.

In the world of thought, we find the concept of 'chance'.[6] Chance is the part of a thing that cannot be deduced, reduced, or destroyed. It is what makes every thing equally something, neither *more* nor *less* than anything else. Considering the chance of every thing makes it possible to represent the world as an equal world, one lacking all intensity and resistant to the incessant variations of our lives. Only such an equal conception of this equal thing gives us a way of counteracting the intensities to which our existence is constantly exposed. It would be wrong to use this to *negate* our character as living beings instead of using it as a means of *resistance*. Resistance means both refusing to say yes and refusing to say no. Being ethical consists of hanging in there and using a sort of immobility to mount an opposition to the continuous flow of life. This immobility finds expression in words and ideas as well as in the identities that we extract from our ever-changing sensations. The thinking part of our selves is brought into crashing confrontation with fluctuating perceptions, polymorphous desires, and our own internal electricity, and that clash makes it possible for us to hope that palpably experiencing it will make us feel alive. Thought can put up a dam, but when it breaks, the current carries everything away. All too soon, the lack of resistance causes the absolute movement of life to start to feel like something permanent, inert, and routine. But if, on the other hand, thought manages to entirely stop, control, and command the current of our nature, the rushing white water then sleepily coalesces into dead water. The intensity of the living becomes nothing but a stagnant pool of being. Such a life is eternal, and it has found the path to salvation, but it ends up being inert all the same.

The force of a life is a very delicate thing. To feel alive for as long as possible, we have to toe the line between ideas and sensations. We have to resist giving in to life in a kind of vertiginous affirmation, but we also have to struggle not to fall into the abyss of life's negation. Affirming life too much will only negate it, but negating life is not the same as affirming it. Such negation is just a slightly perverse way of turning the power of life against itself. Beings that live and think always lose unless they carefully manage the powerful current that they feel coursing through them. Their thinking ends up neutralising what is strongest in their being. Sentient life has this chance: there is something in the way that we feel that cannot be reduced to anything else. It is the secret treasure within every being that feels, the pearl at the heart of my sensations, the part of me that is mine and mine alone. It is the feeling of not being a lifeless, universal observer spying on the living.

What more can we ask of life than to be permitted to work at sustaining the feeling that makes it lively? That feeling is never guaranteed, but everyone must be able to hope to maintain it for a period of time. For a sentient, intelligent being, nothing is more intense than finding a way to think without nullifying the chance of being alive.

Notes

1. Čapek, *R.U.R.*, p. 65.
2. *Form and Object*'s Book II, Chapter VI: 'Humans' describes the process that first led humans to try to teach language to non-human animals, and then to try to create artificial machine minds. On the traditional view, humans occupied the metaphysical niche between God and animals. We tried to make ourselves more God-like precisely when faith in the traditional Judeo-Christian God (who creates life and doles out language) had weakened, which is to say, precisely when we had begun to understand ourselves as animals. Chimpanzee sign language and artificial intelligence were both products of humanity's desperate metaphysical gambit to preserve itself as distinct from

(because God-like with respect to) supposedly (that is, according to dominant strains in Western metaphysics) material entities such as animals and machines.

3. Garcia's use of this Sartrean phrase (cf. Sartre's *Existentialism is a Humanism*) is an absolutely clear indication that this passage is (at the very least) targeting marketplace existentialism as a key instance of thinking that attempts to defend life from being thought.

4. See Chapter 6 note 1 on Garcia's related notions of 'chance' and 'price to pay'.

5. This is a segue into the next book in Garcia's trilogy, *Nous*.

6. In asserting the right of every thing to its chance, or at least insisting that such an assertion is necessary, this concluding passage echoes the restoration of the ontological dignity of all things that under-pins Garcia's philosophical project. Furthermore, by referring to the language of 'chance', Garcia is also here invoking the language of the 'chance and the price' that he employs in the concluding moments of *Form and Object*. The formal homologies between *Form and Object* and this work have been discussed in the Translators' Introduction, but in this final stretch they also provide a clue as to how we might deal with the apparent aporia that we have now encountered. Essentially, as Garcia intimates in the final Coda of *Form and Object*, the thinking accomplished in both of these works remains imperfect, incomplete, and therefore all the more vibrant. What we are left with is a paradoxical preparation for the failure of our own thinking that nevertheless insists that finding a way to think and live is indispensable. Some kinds of thinking leave us at the end of a road, and other kinds signal the way forward on a path yet to be explored. However, the situation we find ourselves in at the end of this work is altogether different: our final position is undecided, interstitial, and persists, up in the air, like an acrobat on a tightrope.

Bibliography

Adorno, Theodor W., *Aesthetic Theory*, trans. Robert Hullor-Kentor, London: Continuum, 2004.

Aristotle, *Categories (Chapters 1–5)*, trans. J. L. Ackrill, https://faculty.washington.edu/smcohen/ 520/Cats1-5.pdf (last accessed 12 October 2017).

Barine, Arvède, 'Essais de littérature pathologique: L'Opium – Thomas De Quincey (Première partie)', *Revue des deux mondes* 38 (1896), pp. 116–46.

Baudelaire, Charles, *Les Fleurs du Mal*, ed. John E. Jackson, Paris: Librairie Générale Française, 1999.

Baudrillard, Jean, 'Entretien réalisé par Raphaël Bessis et Lucas Degryse', interview by Raphaël Bessis and Lucas Degryse, *Le Philosophoire* (2003), https://www.cairn.info/revue-le-philosophoire-2003-1-page-5.html (last accessed 3 November 2017).

Beiser, Frederick, *The Fate of Reason: German Philosophy from Kant to Fichte*, Cambridge, MA: Harvard University Press, 1993.

Beiser, Frederick, *German Idealism: The Struggle against Subjectivism, 1781–1801*, Cambridge, MA: Harvard University Press, 2008.

Beiser, Frederick, *Hegel*, London: Routledge, 2005.

Bennett, Jonathan, *Kant's Analytic*, Cambridge: Cambridge University Press, 1966.

Berdyaev, Nicolas, *The Destiny of Man*, trans. Natalie Duddington, New York: Harper & Brothers, 1960.

Braver, Lee, *A Thing of This World: A History of Continental Anti-Realism*, Chicago: Northwestern University Press, 2007.

Bryant, Levi, *The Democracy of Objects*, Ann Arbor, MI: Open Humanities Press, 2011.

Buzaglo, Meir, *Solomon Maimon: Monism, Skepticism, and Mathematics*, Pittsburgh: University of Pittsburgh Press, 2002.

Byron, George Gordon, Lord, 'Stanzas Composed During a Thunderstorm', *Bartleby.com*, http://www.bartleby.com/205/6.html (last accessed 25 October 2017).

Čapek, Karel, *R.U.R. (Rossum's Universal Robot) & The Robber*, trans. Voyen Koreis, Brisbane: Booksplendour Publishing, 2008.

Chabot, Pascal, *Global Burn-out*, Paris: Presses Universitaires de France, 2013.

Chateaubriand, François, *Atala, René, Les aventures du dernier Abencérage*, ed. Jean-Claude Berchet, Paris: Flammarion, 1996.

Cogburn, Jon, 'Aesthetics as First Philosophy: Sense Making after Speculative Realism', http://www.academia.edu/22685785/Aesthetics_as_First_Philosophy_Sense_Making_After_Speculative_Realism (last accessed 4 December 2017).

Cogburn, Jon, '#DECELERATE MANIFESTO: for a Decelerationist Anti-Politics', *Philosophical Percolations* (June 2015), http://www.philpercs.com/2015/06/decelerate-manifesto-for-a-decelerationist-anti-politics.html (last accessed 3 November 2017).

Cogburn, Jon, *Garcian Meditations: The Dialectics of Persistence in* Form and Object, Edinburgh: Edinburgh University Press, 2017.

Cogburn, Jon, Review of *Gilbert Simondon: Being and Technology*, ed. Arne De Boever, Alex Murray, Jon Roffe, and Ashley Woodward, *Notre Dame Philosophical Reviews* (2013), http://ndpr.nd.edu/news/gilbert-simondon-being-and-technology/ (last accessed 5 December 2017).

Cogburn, Jon, and Mark Silcox, 'The Emergence of Emergence: Computability and Ontology', *American Philosophical Quarterly* 48:1 (2011), pp. 63–74.

Cogburn, Jon, and Franklin Worrell, 'S-Vagueness and R-Vagueness: Some Results from Counterexamples to the Underlying Comparative Theory', https://www.academia.edu/18797604/S-Vagueness_and_R-Vagueness_Some_results_from_counterexamples_to_ the_underlying_comparative_theory (last accessed 22 November 2015).

Condillac, Étienne Bonnot, *Traité des sensations* (1754), *fr.wikisource. org*, https://fr.wikisource.org/wiki/Trait%C3%A9_des_sensations/Premi%C3%A8re_partie (last accessed 11 November 2017).

Crary, Jonathan, *24/7: Late Capitalism and the Ends of Sleep*, New York: Verso, 2014.

d'Alembert, Jean le Rond, Edme-François Mallet, and Arnulphe d'Aumont, 'Génération', in *Encyclopédie, ou dictionnaire raisonné des sciences, des arts et des métiers, etc.*, ed. Denis Diderot and Jean le Rond d'Alembert, University of Chicago: ARTFL Encyclopédie Project (Spring 2016), ed. Robert Morrissey and Glenn Roe, http://encyclopedie.uchicago.edu/.

Darnton, Robert, *Mesmerism and the End of the Enlightenment in France*, Cambridge, MA: Harvard University Press, 2009.

De Beauvoir, Simone, *Mémoires d'une jeune fille rangée*, Paris: Éditions Gallimard, 1958.

De Laclos, Pierre Choderlos, *Les Liaisons dangereuses*, Paris: J. Rozez, 1869, https://fr. wikisource.org/wiki/Les_Liaisons_dangereuses (last accessed 14 November 2017).

De Morency, Suzanne G. (Suzanne Quinquet), *Illyrine ou L'écueil de l'inexpérience*, Paris: S. Quinquet, an VII, 1798–99.

De Musset, Alfred, *Lorenzaccio*, Paris: Charpentier, IV, 1888, https://fr.wikisource.org/wiki/ Lorenzaccio/Acte_I (last accessed 14 November 2017).

De Quincey, Thomas, *Coleridge and Opium-Eating and Other Writings*, Edinburgh: Adam and Charles Black, 1862.

De Sèze, Paul-Victor, *Recherches phisiologiques et philosophiques sur la sensibilité ou la vie animale*, Paris: Chez Théophile Barrois le jeune, 1786.

De Staël, Germaine, *Lettres sur les écrits et le caractère de Jean-Jacques Rousseau*, Clermont-Ferrand: Éditions Paleo, 2014.

Deleuze, Gilles, 'How Do We Recognize Structuralism?' (2002), in *Desert Islands and Other Texts, 1953–1974*, trans. David Lapoujade, ed. Michael Taormina, Los Angeles: Semiotext(e), 2004.

Delon, Michel, *L'Idée d'énergie au tournant des Lumières*, Paris: Presses Universitaires de France, 1988.

Deprun, Jean, 'Sade et la rationalisme des Lumières', in *Raison Présente* 3, Paris: Éditions Rationalistes, 1967, pp. 75–90.

Descartes, René, *The Passions of the Soul*, trans. Stephen Voss, Cambridge: Hackett, 1989.

Dick, Philip K., *Do Androids Dream of Electric Sheep?*, New York: Del Rey, 1996.

Dransfeld, Klaus, Paul Kienle, and Georg Michael Kalvius, *Physik I: Mechanik und Wärme*, Munich: Oldenbourg Wissenschaftsverlag, 2005.

Ehrenberg, Alain, *The Weariness of the Self*, trans. Enrico Caouette, Jacob Homel, David Homel, and Don Winkler, under the direction of David Homel, Montreal: McGill-Queens University Press, 2010.

Floury, Nicolas, *De l'usage addictif: Une ontologie du sujet toxicomane*, Paris: Les Contemporains favoris, 2016.

Galvani, Luigi Aloisio, *De viribus electricitatis in motu musculari*, Bologna: Ex typographia Instituti Scientiarum, 1791.

Garcia, Tristan, *Forme et objet: Un traité des choses*, Paris: Presses Universitaires de France, 2011.

Garcia, Tristan, *Form and Object: A Theory of Things*, trans. Mark Allan Ohm and Jon Cogburn, Edinburgh: Edinburgh University Press, 2014.

Garcia, Tristan, *Nous*, Paris: Bernard Grasset, 2016.

Garcia, Tristan, *La Vie Intense: Une obsession moderne*, Paris: Autrement, 2016.

Garnier, Philippe, *La tiédeur*, Paris: Presses Universitaires de France, 2000.

Gendler, Tamar, and John Hawthorne (eds), *Conceivability and Possibility*, Oxford: Clarendon Press, 2002.

Goethe, Johann Wolfgang, *The Sorrows of Young Werther: Elective Affinities*, trans. R. D. Boylan, ed. Nathen Haskell Dole, CreateSpace Independent Publishing Platform, 2015.

Guillerme, André, 'L'électricité dans ses premiers grandeurs (1760–1820)', *Revue d'histoire des sciences* 54:1 (2001), pp. 5–9.

Han, Byung-Chul, *The Burnout Society*, Stanford: Stanford University Press, 2015.

Hankins, Thomas, *Jean d'Alembert: Science and the Enlightenment*, Oxford: Clarendon Press, 1970.

Harman, Graham, *Guerrilla Metaphysics: Phenomenology and the Carpentry of Things*, Chicago: Open Court, 2005.

Harman, Graham, 'Object-Oriented France: The Philosophy of Tristan Garcia', *continent* 2:1 (2012), pp. 6–21.

Harman, Graham, *Prince of Networks: Bruno Latour and Metaphysics*, Melbourne: re.press, 2009.

Harman, Graham, *The Quadruple Object*, Washington, DC: Zero Books, 2011.

Harman, Graham, *Quentin Meillassoux: Philosophy in the Making*, 2nd edn, Edinburgh: Edinburgh University Press, 2015.

Harman, Graham, *Tool-Being: Heidegger and the Metaphysics of Objects*, Chicago: Open Court, 2002.

Harman, Graham, *Towards Speculative Realism: Essays and Lectures*, Washington, DC: Zero Books, 2010.

Harman, Graham, 'Tristan Garcia and the Thing-in-itself', *Parrhesia: A Journal of Critical Philosophy* 16 (2013), pp. 26–34.

Harman, Graham, 'Whitehead and Schools X, Y, and Z', in *The Lure of Whitehead*, ed. Nicholas Gaskill and Adam Nocek, Minneapolis: University of Minnesota Press, 2014.

Hegel, G. W. F., *Encyclopedia of the Philosophical Sciences in Basic Outline, Part 1, Science of Logic*, trans. Klaus Brinkmann and Daniel Dahlstrohm, Cambridge: Cambridge University Press, 2015.

Hegel, G. W. F., *Phenomenology of Spirit*, trans. A. V. Miller, Oxford: Oxford University Press, 1977.

Hegel, G. W. F., *The Science of Logic*, trans. George Di Giovanni, Cambridge: Cambridge University Press, 2015.

Heller, Joshua, and Jon Cogburn, 'Meillassoux's Dilemma', https://www.academia.edu/ 18797280/MEILLASSOUX_S_DILEMMA_PARADOXES_OF_TOTALITY_AFTER_THE_SPECULATIVE_TURN (last accessed 22 November 2015).

Hugo, Victor, 'Soleil Couchant', in *A Sheaf Gleaned in French Fields*, ed. and trans. Toru Dutt, London: Kegan Paul, 1880, https://en.wikisource.org/wiki/A_Sheaf_Gleaned_in_French_ Fields (last accessed 11 November 2017).

Ildefonse, Frédérique, *La naissance de la grammaire dans l'Antiquité grecque*, Paris: Libraire Philosophique J. Vrin, 1997.

Kacem, Mehdi Belhaj, *Algèbre de la Tragédie: Postface de Tristan Garcia: Critique et rémission*, Paris: Editions Léo Scheer, 2014.

Kant, Immanuel, *Critique of Pure Reason*, trans. Warner Pluhar, Indianapolis: Hackett, 1996.

Kierkegaard, Søren, *The Present Age and Of the Difference between a Genius and an Apostle*, trans. Alexander Dru, New York: Harper Torchbooks, 1940.

Ladyman, James, 'Structural Realism', *Stanford Encyclopedia of Philosophy* (2014), https://plato.stanford.edu/entries/structural-realism/#OthStr (last accessed 24 October 2017).

Lewis, C. S., *The Abolition of Man*, New York: HarperOne, 2015.

Livingston, Paul, *The Politics of Logic: Badiou, Wittgenstein, and the Consequences of Formalism*, London: Routledge, 2014.

Livy, *History of Rome, Volume VI, Books 23–25*, trans. Frank Gardner Moore, Loeb Classical Library 355, Cambridge, MA: Harvard University Press, 1940.

Mader, Mary Beth, 'Whence Intensity? Deleuze and the Revival of a Concept', in *Deleuze and Metaphysics*, ed. Alain Beaulieu, Ed Kazarian, and Julia Sushytska, Lanham, MD: Rowman and Littlefield, 2014.

Maimon, Salomon, *Essay on Transcendental Philosophy*, London: Bloomsbury Academic, 2010.

Marcuse, Herbert, *One-Dimensional Man*, Boston: Beacon Press, 1964.

McDowell, John, *Mind and World*, Cambridge, MA: Harvard University Press, 1996.

Meillassoux, Quentin, *After Finitude: An Essay on the Necessity of Contingency*, New York: Bloomsbury Academic, 2010.

Moore, A. W., *The Evolution of Modern Metaphysics: Making Sense of Things*, Cambridge: Cambridge University Press, 2012.

Newton, Isaac, *The Principia: The Authoritative Translation and Guide: Mathematical Principles of Natural Philosophy Paperback*, trans. Bernard Cohen, Anne Whitman, and Julia Budenz, Berkeley: University of California Press, 2016.

Nietzsche, Friedrich, 'On Truth and Lies in a Extra-Moral Sense', in *The Portable Nietzsche*, trans. Walter Kaufmann, London: Penguin Books, 1977, pp. 42–6.

Nietzsche, Friedrich, *The Will to Power*, trans. Walter Kaufmann and R. J. Hollingsdale, ed. Walter Kaufmann, New York: Vintage Books, 1968.

Pichon, Georges, *Le morphinisme: impulsions délictueuses, troubles physiques et mentaux des morphinomanes, leur capacité et leur situation juridique: cause, déontologie et prophylaxie du vice morphinique*, Paris: O. Doin, 1889.

Plato, *Cratylus*, in *Plato: The Collected Dialogues*, ed. Edith Hamilton and Huntington Cairns, Princeton: Princeton University Press, 1989.

Poincaré, Henri, *Science and Hypothesis*, London: Walter Scott Publishing, 1905.

Pollock, Konstantin, 'The "Transcendental Method": On the Reception of the *Critique of Pure Reason* in Neo-Kantianism', in *The Cambridge Companion to Kant's Critique of Pure Reason*, ed. Paul Guyer, Cambridge: Cambridge University Press, 2010.

Priest, Graham, *Beyond the Limits of Thought*, Oxford: Oxford University Press, 2002.

Proust, Marcel, *In Search of Lost Time, Volume I, Swann's Way*, trans. C. K. Scott Moncrieff and Terence Kilmartin, New York: The Modern Library, 1992.

Purnell, Carolyn, *The Sensational Past: How the Enlightenment Changed How We Use Our Senses*, New York: W. W. Norton, 2017.

Rimbaud, Arthur, 'Adieu', in *A Season in Hell and The Drunken Boat*, trans. Louise Varèse, New York: New Directions, 1961.

Rimbaud, Arthur, *Illuminations, and Other Prose Poems*, trans. Louise Varèse, New York: New Directions, 1957.

Routier, Guillaume, and Bastien Soulé, 'Jouer avec la gravité: approche sociologique plurielle de l'engagement dans des sports dangereux', *Sociologies* (June 2010), http://sociologies. revues.org/3121 (last accessed 3 November 2017).

Sade, Donatien Alphonse François, Marquis de, *Philosophy in the Bedroom* (1795), trans. Richard Seaver and Austryn Wainhouse, http://www.sin.org/tales/Marquis_de_Sade--Philosophy_in_ the_Bedroom.pdf (last accessed 25 October 2017).

Sartre, Jean Paul, *Existentialism is a Humanism*, trans. Carol Macomber, New Haven, CT: Yale University Press, 2007.

Schmiechen, Michael, *Newton's Principia Revisited*, Berlin: BOD, 2009.

Sève, Bernard, *L'Altération musicale: Ou ce que la musique apprend au philosophe*, Paris: Seuil, 2002.

Shelley, Mary, *Frankenstein*, Mineola, NY: Dover, 1994.

Snetlage, Leonhard, *Nouveau dictionnaire français contenant les expressions de nouvelle création du peuple français: Ouvrage additionnel au Dictionnaire de l'Académie Française et de tout autre vocabulaire*, Göttingen: Jean Chrêtien Dietrich Libraire, 1795.

Toulet, Paul-Jean, *Les Contrerimes: poèmes*, Paris: Édition Émile-Paul frères, 1929, https://fr.wikisource.org/wiki/Les_Contrerimes (last accessed 14 November 2017).

Unamuno, Miguel, *The Tragic Sense of Life in Men and Nations*, Princeton: Princeton University Press, 1978.

Verlaine, Paul, 'Monsieur Prudhomme', in *Poèmes saturniens*, Paris: Vanier, 1902, https://fr. wikisource.org/wiki/Po%C3%A8mes_ saturniens/Monsieur_Prudhomme (last accessed 11 November 2017).

Whitehead, Alfred North, *Process and Reality: An Essay in Cosmology*, Cambridge: Cambridge University Press, 1929.

Williams, Alex, and Nick Srnicek, '#ACCELERATE MANIFESTO: for an Accelerationist Politics', *Critical Legal Thinking* (May 2013), http://criticallegalthinking.com/2013/05/14/ accelerate-manifesto-for-an-accelerationist-politics/ (last accessed 3 November 2017).

Index

Page numbers followed by 'n' refer to notes, and those followed by 't' refer to tables.